9

4

4

Am I Teaching Well?

Lisa Hayes
Vesna Nikolic
Hanna Cabaj

Learning Matters

Original edition first published in 2000 by Pippin Publishing Corporation.
UK edition first published in 2001 by Learning Matters Ltd.

Original edition written by Vesna Nikolic and Hanna Cabaj.

Original edition © Pippin Publishing Corporation
All new material for the UK edition © Lisa Hayes

British Library Cataloguing in Publication Data
A CIP record for this book is available from the British Library

ISBN 1 903300 30 4

Illustrated by Pat Cupples
Project Management by Deer Park Productions
Typeset by PDQ Typesetting
Printed and bound in Great Britain by Bell & Bain Ltd., Glasgow

Learning Matters Ltd
58 Wonford Road
Exeter EX2 4LQ
Tel: 01392 215560
Email: info@learningmatters.co.uk
www.learningmatters.co.uk

To be a more effective teacher is a goal shared by most, if not all teachers. This book provides strategies and ideas that encourage active reflection on teaching styles and practices. This active reflection will enable practising and training teachers to identify their strengths and capitalise on them, and highlight any weaknesses so that they can be addressed.

This book is intended to meet the needs of experienced, newly qualified and student teachers who wish to explore and develop their own ideas. It will also be of use to those working with teachers in developing skills, school managers, governors and those involved in initial teacher training and continuing professional development.

This book is not intended to be read from cover to cover, instead it employs a modular approach. The first chapter concentrates on highlighting strengths, weaknesses and areas for improvement. The chapters can then be explored in any sequence according to the needs of each individual teacher. Each of the tasks involves the ability to observe and think critically about one's own actions. This can be done through self-reflection or through self-reflection combined with video- or audio-taping, peer observation, or other techniques as described in Chapter 1. Teachers can use the tasks and the process of self-reflection to build a collection of self-evaluation data. This data can then be used to evidence professional development and build a professional development record.

From the authors of the original edition

We are delighted to see a new edition of our book reaching our colleagues in Britain. As Lisa Hayes explained in her preface, commitment to self-evaluation in teaching helps us reach our full potential by identifying our strengths and weaknesses. If systematic reflection on our practice becomes a guiding principle of our professional lives, we are more likely to achieve our goals. Even though the series of small-scale experiments in this book may only scratch the surface of our teaching skills, it could mark the beginning of a career-long endeavour.

We have been fortunate to have met many fine educators throughout our careers whose credos were similar to those advocated in this book. The book could never have been started – much less finished – were it not for their direct and indirect contributions. Many thanks go to Leo Lynch, Esther Podoliak, Slawomir Wysokinski, Michael Galli and Lisa Morgan for their encouragement and suggestions. We also wish to acknowledge the wonderful team of the Toronto Catholic District School Board Adult Education Program, and highlight all we have learned from our own teachers and students in Canada, Croatia and Poland, and from the authors in the bibliography and resource list, whose work has been a source of insight and inspiration.

Our deepest gratitude goes to our children Marko and Martina Nikolic, and Alexandra Cabaj, and our husbands, Ivica and Peter. This book is the tangible evidence of their unflagging love and support.

Finally, we would like to dedicate this book to our parents in Croatia and Poland, for teaching us the value and joy of work.

Vesna Nikolic
Hanna Cabaj
Toronto, August 2001

Why self-evaluate?

The response to this question is simple: no professional can acquire the skills of a peak performer without absolute willingness constantly to assess, explore, examine, and improve their practice.

Consider this scenario, familiar to all teachers: during a lesson, one of your pupils asks for clarification. What would you select as the best course of action?

- Respond only to that pupil, looking at and talking to him or her alone.
- Repeat the question for everyone in class, and then address it.
- Repeat the question for everyone in class, and then ask if anyone knows the answer.
- Put off addressing the question until later, because you do not want to disrupt your lesson.

And while you are responding, where would you be standing?

- Next to the pupil who asked the question;
- At a position in the class where everyone can see you;
- Somewhere else.

Does it matter which of these options you choose? And do you ask yourself similar questions every day? If you do, you are one of those teachers who constantly strives to develop and improve teaching practice.

Evaluation seems to be part of human nature, part of an innate need to make judgments and express opinions. We evaluate others, formally or informally, but we also engage regularly in self-evaluation of our behaviour, personal as well as professional. Evaluation is an integral part of the teaching process. We evaluate our teaching practice to inform our decisions about planning and organisation. Some of us also encourage pupils to evaluate our teaching and offer feedback, even if only informally.

Most of teachers' daily work is determined by judgments, decisions, and choices. Some of these are 'macro' decisions, so crucial that they can make or break a class. Others, such as deciding on ways to answer a student's question, are related to micro teaching skills; they may not be critical, but they play a significant role in the classroom. The results of these major decisions and the fine-tuning of choices distinguish a weak, mediocre, or solid teacher from a peak performer.

Due to the fact that the quality of teaching depends on decisions and choices, interest in self-assessment in teaching is growing. The importance and popularity of classroom research and teacher self-evaluation have increased rapidly since the 1950s. Self-evaluation is now a standard component of staff performance evaluation in most education systems.

In a 1982 paper, Donald Freeman proposes an implicit hierarchy of issues that teachers face as they move from the training to the development stage of professional growth.

For novice teachers, the primary and dominant question is 'What do I teach?'. As teachers gain experience, the *what* question gives way to 'How do I teach?' and an exploration of ways and means of working with learners. Finally, once the *whats* and *hows* cease to pose difficulties, we enter the third stage of our development and begin to ask ourselves, 'Why do I teach what I teach, and why do I teach it the way I do?'. This progression applies not only to novice teachers' journey to experience, but also to teachers with years of experience who face new teaching situations – a new curriculum, or a new group of pupils.

Freeman's *what, how,* and *why* questions are part of a process of decision-making and reflection that we engage in on an ongoing basis throughout our careers. How we go about answering these questions and developing our practice is quite idiosyncratic. Many components of effective teaching could be identified, but there is no magic formula that works for all educators. The only thing you can always say about teaching is 'That depends on a number of factors…'. We all bring unique personalities, skills, preferences, and aptitudes into our classrooms, and so do our pupils. One teacher's most effective activity might be a weak point for another and overkill for a third. We do not all have to have the same understanding of methodology and practice.

In the light of these differences, it would be absurd for us to prescribe recipes, claiming that they work equally well for every teacher in every class. Instead, we offer a variety of options. As readers work through the tasks we describe, they should consider their particular pupils, their teaching context, their own personality traits, and specifics of their curricula – to name just a few variables.

The benefits of self-evaluation

One of the goals of many teacher support and inservice programmes is to provide teachers with tools that direct and facilitate reflection. It is through such processes that teachers grow. Teachers who are already 'converted' do not need to be convinced of this; they know that self-evaluation is highly beneficial. As for sceptics, we hope that this list of the benefits of self-evaluation will persuade them to join the many teachers who already engage in this process:

- self-evaluation facilitates learning and development of self-knowledge;
- it directs professional development and career planning, with resulting increases in professional satisfaction;
- it enhances feelings of job security and opens the door to growth and promotion opportunities;
- it arms teachers with tools for raising their awareness about their teaching and identifying problem areas;
- it ensures systematic and ongoing work on improving teaching patterns;
- it helps teachers better comprehend and articulate the rationales behind classroom behaviours, activities, and events.

The benefits for departments and schools include:

- it ensures systematic work on professional growth;
- it promotes professional development, but still allows for individual differences;

- it renders staff evaluation more collaborative and participatory;
- it ensures quality of delivery;
- as a group project, it fosters growth in the entire department or school and enhances collegiality;
- it reduces the need for formal management evaluation.

Techniques for self-evaluation

All teachers self-evaluate, but most do so subconsciously and informally. A systematic approach to analysing what is happening in the classroom is preferable to occasional reflection, however, and can lead to concrete ideas for improvement.

Our model for systematic self-evaluation, outlined in Figure 1, reflects the stages teachers may go through as they work with the collection of tasks in this book. Self-evaluation can involve many techniques. Those described in what follows are some common approaches, many of which are discussed in more detail later. Results can best be achieved by adopting a 'combination' approach – that is, by using two or more of the techniques simultaneously – to yield deeper insight than is possible with any single technique.

Personal reflection: diaries or journals

Through reflective writing in journals or diaries, teachers can express their feelings about their teaching, working environment, relationship with pupils, concerns, and successes. Written candidly immediately or shortly after a lesson, entries in a teaching

Raising awareness
  self-evaluation
  questionnaires and checklists
  professional development

Modifying and improving teaching practice:
  writing accounts of findings
  defining goals for future

development

Establishing a systematic process of self-observation
  self-monitoring combined with video-
  and audio-taping or peer observation

Ensuring systematic observation
and analysis of findings:
  evaluating the impact of

changes in the classroom
identifying how certain aspects of
teaching practice have improved

The systematic process of self-evaluation

diary present personal accounts of the teaching activities, observations, and reflections, and views of how the classroom experience affects teachers' professional and personal lives. The entries can then be analysed for recurring patterns or salient events. The professional literature has long recognised the effectiveness of keeping a teaching diary or journal for purposes of self-evaluation.

Action research: classroom tasks, action plans

Action research, a form of reflective inquiry, has been employed in professional development in education for well over forty years. It links theory and practice, providing an effective way for teachers to try out ideas in the classroom to increase their knowledge about the curriculum, teaching, and learning. A typical action research project goes through stages of reconnaissance, planning, action, observation, and reflection. It can be conducted individually or within a team, with or without pupil involvement; it is based in a real situation, is highly participatory, and enables productive self-evaluation.

Self-reporting: checklists or questionnaires

Many teachers conduct self-evaluation through questionnaires and checklists, although no practical guide that discusses all aspects of teaching seems to exist for this approach. To some extent, we hope this book addresses this lack.

The advantage of questionnaires and checklists is that they can be answered and their findings analysed in a non-threatening environment. The ultimate goals of questionnaires are to raise the respondent's awareness and to promote self-observation; if this is achieved, the checklists serve their purpose well. Their shortcoming lies in the lack of objectivity of the responses – we are all prone to responding in a much more positive light than that of truth and reality.

We believe that, despite this limitation, questionnaires and checklists can be an effective component of self-evaluation if they are used in conjunction with other techniques – notably video- and audio-taping or peer observation. This involves time and commitment, but the outcomes can be highly beneficial.

Self-observation: audio- or video-recording of lessons

Audio- or video-recording of lessons is the most reliable and accurate means of documenting what actually happens in the classroom. One way of using this procedure for self-evaluation is to record lessons for a one- or two-week period, with the goal of capturing as much class interaction as possible. Tapes can then be selected at random for analysis.

Professional development records

Professional development records are gaining popularity as a self-evaluation technique. Portfolios are collections of materials assembled to be representative of work accomplished in a particular subject, with a particular group of learners, or in an entire school year. They may include lesson plans, student work samples, records of activities outside the classroom, records of courses taken, summaries of professional books and articles, notes from students or their parents, name tags from workshops or conferences, photos, videos, and so on. The contents may be reviewed with a line manager or peer during an evaluation meeting. New systems of evaluation implemented under performance management will benefit from the evidence that can be provided by a professional development records. Similarly all newly qualified teachers require a career entry profile that can be completed using some of the tasks in the following chapters.

Peer observation

To see what is happening in the classroom more clearly – particularly if access to video- or audio-taping is not available – teachers may need assistance from their colleagues. Peer observation has long been considered conducive to teacher learning, especially if the teacher observed is an experienced one and the observation is followed by conferences and analysis of findings.

Over the years, ideas for peer observation have been revised and new methods and possibilities have been developed. Observation can be conducted in pairs or groups; a second observer may be invited to class to ensure objectivity; all parties may write diary entries or fill out checklists or observation report forms to elicit all perceptions of the lesson. Whatever the form, the value of peer observation comes not only in learning gained by the observer through watching another teacher's methods, but also in follow-up sessions. It is in post-observation discussions that we draw conclusions that help improve our teaching patterns and boost our professional growth.

In general, when done systematically and seriously, peer observation is a beneficial process for all participants. Even though it may be time-consuming and costly if used as a staff-development technique, it has many advantages: it is participatory, democratic, and less threatening than management observation and evaluation. For more objective results, it may be combined with video evaluation.

Continuing professional development (CPD)

Teachers and schools are now required to evidence staff professional development. This means that teachers are encouraged to state objectives for professional growth in different areas of teaching and to reflect on the results at the end of the designated period. The tasks provided in this book can focus and facilitate this process.

Group professional development projects

This technique involves the whole department or school working with various self-evaluation techniques together. The senior management team can and should do a great deal to encourage teachers to participate in such projects by presenting the idea, making any necessary timetable changes to ensure that teachers get release time for self-evaluation, facilitating workshops and sessions that clarify the techniques proposed for use, and organising events that not all teachers can organise on their own (video or portfolio evaluation, for example). We are all certainly more motivated to engage in self-evaluation projects if our colleagues are involved, if we can create 'communities of practice' (Moon *et al.*, 2000), and if the project can be accommodated within our busy schedules.

Area of teaching practice	I feel very comfortable with this	I feel least comfortable with this	This is one of my strengths	This is one of my weaknesses	I want to develop this further
My relationship with colleagues Chapter 2					
My classroom organisation Chapter 3					
My relationships with pupils Chapter 3					
My role in the classroom Chapter 3					
My schemes of work Chapter 4					
My lesson planning Chapter 5					
My use of effective and varied teaching strategies Chapters 5 & 7					
My use of resources Chapter 6					
My variety of classroom communication Chapter 8					
My questioning technique Chapter 9					
The motivation and attitude of my pupils Chapter 10					
My feedback to pupils Chapter 11					
My use of assessment techniques Chapter 12					
My evaluation of what I am teaching Chapter 13					
My continuing professional development Chapter 14					

Management Evaluation

Practitioners and theorists alike agree on the importance and value of self-assessment. Agreement on the need for formal management evaluation, however, might be a more contentious issue. Of course all teachers are subject to Ofsted inspectors observing their lessons, but may find this stressful.

Teachers often point out that no one can pass judgment on their teaching without a broader understanding of their classes, pupils, and other factors that only they possess. Also, the presence of an observer changes the classroom atmosphere and teaching situation significantly.

Obviously, the strategies used for conducting teacher evaluation have to be carefully selected, and managers need to be sensitive to teachers' concerns.

Identify your strengths and weaknesses

Teachers self-evaluate in different ways. Each teacher has his or her own priorities for areas that need improvement; in addition, subjects are not identical in the emphasis they place on various aspects of teaching, nor do all departments base their expectations on the same elements. Since this book attempts to present a thorough guide to self-monitoring over a range of teaching aspects, readers should select tasks related to the areas that they or their departments or schools wish to focus on.

The following tasks, however, are recommended for all readers. They provide an introduction to the process of self-evaluation and are intended to help you identify particular areas on which you might choose to concentrate.

TASK 1

Conducting a systematic, critical analysis of your own classroom performance takes courage. It involves a willingness to criticise your current teaching habits and requires openness to the spirit of change. Think about your determination to improve your teaching practice and to reflect on your views with the ultimate goal of changing your teaching patterns.

1 How willing are you to start a systematic process of self-analysis, instead of undertaking only casual observation?

2 If you are uncertain that you are willing to embark on systematic self-evaluation, identify your reasons.

3 How legitimate are these reasons?

TASK 2

Take some time to look through the tasks in this book. As you do, complete the checklist opposite to identify your ideas of strength and weakness and highlight areas you would like to develop:

1 When you have completed this use your answers to identify the weak areas you would like to work on first and begin working through the relevant chapter.

Summary

In this first chapter we have introduced some techniques for self-evaluation that you can use to reflect on your teaching practice. The tasks in this chapter will have given you time to reflect on your feelings about the process of self-evaluation, will have indicated strengths and weaknesses in your teaching practice and given you a focus area for development. A copy of the checklist for Task 2 would be useful evidence for your professional development record. You could re-do the checklist after a certain time (e.g. a term or a year) and include student work, lesson plans, schemes of work or details of training sessions attended, to provide evidence of development in a particular weak area.

Teachers' working environments vary greatly. The nature of the contact teachers have with one another and with other education professionals is determined by a number of factors.

We all appreciate working in a supportive and friendly group. It is well accepted that a congenial atmosphere is one of the foundations of a healthy work environment. Sharing, partnership, good will, and friendship not only strengthen professional ties but are beneficial for well-being both in and out of the workplace. Many schools can boast exemplary staff cooperation, where teachers are on the same wavelengths and all contribute to the growth of their school. In others, staff coexist with politeness and form groups of compatible individuals. In still others, teachers openly express resentment and bitterness, and needling appears to be the only form of communication.

Why do some groups coexist and cooperate flawlessly while others are beset by personality and professional conflicts? Is it possible to create a team from inherently incompatible individuals? These questions reveal complicated issues that baffle many school management teams. We all have a responsibility to do our part in creating a positive atmosphere in the workplace. This chapter will help you identify the challenges of staffroom interaction and encourage you to think about what you can do to improve collaboration with your colleagues.

The working environment

Successful interaction within any teaching environment implies solid cooperation among colleagues. That cooperation is the basis for collective professional growth. Therefore, it is important that we occasionally reflect upon how we contribute to the atmosphere of our work environment and what we can do to improve that atmosphere as we work side by side with our colleagues.

TASK 1

❶ How do you interact with your colleagues?

	Always				Never
	5	4	3	2	1
We socialise together.	☐	☐	☐	☐	☐
We collaborate.	☐	☐	☐	☐	☐
We support one another.	☐	☐	☐	☐	☐
We act to motivate and inspire one another.	☐	☐	☐	☐	☐
We share and exchange ideas and materials.	☐	☐	☐	☐	☐
We try to resolve conflicts, clear up misunderstandings, and reduce tensions.	☐	☐	☐	☐	☐

We discuss pupils' needs and progress. ☐ ☐ ☐ ☐ ☐

I encourage team work with other staff members. ☐ ☐ ☐ ☐ ☐

I respond to colleagues' initiatives with acknowledgment, praise, and support. ☐ ☐ ☐ ☐ ☐

I participate in all school activities. ☐ ☐ ☐ ☐ ☐

I try not to complain. ☐ ☐ ☐ ☐ ☐

I avoid gossiping about supervisors, students, and

colleagues. ☐ ☐ ☐ ☐ ☐

I do not criticise colleagues, especially less trained or experienced ones. ☐ ☐ ☐ ☐ ☐

I attempt to fit in. ☐ ☐ ☐ ☐ ☐

❷ From the issues mentioned in question 1, identify and analyse one that you feel is a strength and one that is a weakness. Think of some examples and reflect in terms of what you now do or could do to improve collaboration and build stronger professional relationships.

❸ Devise an action plan to implement your ideas about improving the weaknesses you have identified.

TASK 2

❶ By verbalising classroom challenges and successes, we come to a better understanding of ourselves and others. Still, many of us complain that it is difficult to share problems with colleagues, mainly because of fear of losing credibility. How do you feel about this issue?

❷ Think about your reaction when a colleague approaches to share a problem. What do you usually do?

☐ Offer a solution.

☐ I mention that the same thing has happened to me.

☐ I show that I am sympathetic.

☐ I try to come up with suggestions and ways to help.

☐ Other:

❸ When you meet colleagues in the hallway, on duty, at the photocopy machine, or over coffee, do you discuss what they are teaching that day and what their successes or difficulties have been? Do you feel that such sharing is beneficial? Why or why not?

❹ Do you share materials or ideas you have come across and cannot use in your own subject or class but that a colleague might be able to use?

Task 3

Do the following task if you work in a large school, where staff or departmental meetings are held.

❶ How often do you have staff meetings? Are they held during work hours? Do you feel more are needed, or fewer? Why?

❷ Who calls them? Who creates the agenda?

❸ After one of the meetings, review the agenda with your colleagues and identify the issues that were discussed. How relevant or important are they?

❹ Does the choice of issues correspond to staff needs? If not, how could this be changed? What can you do to facilitate such a change?

❺ Do you sometimes suggest agenda items? Why or why not?

❻ Are discussions in staff meetings brief and constructive? If not, what needs to be done?

❼ Do you contribute to discussions? Why or why not?

❽ What (if anything) needs to be changed about these meetings?

Task 4

Regardless of whether you like and/or respect your immediate managers, you may be stuck with them for an extended period. It is crucial to your well-being that you develop positive ways of communicating with senior managers or departmental heads and of avoiding conflict. This can be done by:

- knowing and complying with general rules and policies of the workplace (even the apparently illogical ones usually have some purpose, and fighting them is often pointless in any event);

- being on time (and apologising if an emergency makes you late);

- doing paperwork on schedule;

- being positive, especially in the face of difficulties;

- bringing up suggestions or complaints with discretion and using proper channels;
- keeping a plan and materials for a supply teacher to use in case of emergency or illness.

❶ If you know your manager personally, you may be able to list additional, specific things that could be done to improve communication with her or him. Are there things to which she or he might respond particularly well? What are they?

❷ If your relationship with your line-manager is not what you would like it to be, why is this the case? Is there anything you can do to change it?

❸ Try to recall an incident that caused conflict between you and a manager or colleague. In hindsight, how do you think it could have been avoided?

Task 5

Our pupils carry personal problems and dilemmas with them. Inevitably they bring these through the classroom door.

❶ Getting to know learners' problems and dealing with them is a double-edged sword. Teachers would have to be trained psychologists to fully understand many of these problems. Besides, offering assistance can too often become a burden. On the other hand, if you know nothing about your learners' hardships, you can't assess their implications for the learning process. How do you feel about this issue?

❷ When appropriate, try to assess the relevance of becoming familiar with learners' personal situations. Think of a learner in your class whose situation you know quite well. If you were to walk a mile in his shoes, what challenges would you face? Try to identify at least five.

❸ What implications do these things have for this student's learning process? Does it help that you know the student's situation?

❹ What can you as a teacher do to help this learner?

❺ Are you aware of the economic, family, and social realities others in your class have to face?

Task 6

If you teach adults, your students may be immigrants, refugees, employed or unemployed, welfare recipients, foreign-trained professionals, members of racial or cultural minorities, or parents, and all may be facing different family and social problems. In order to better empathise with your students and support their interests, how do you keep informed of the issues they face?

☐ I talk to students about the challenges they are experiencing.

☐ I talk to colleagues.

☐ I listen to news reports.

☐ I read the newspapers.

☐ Other: _____

Task 7

The teaching community extends beyond the school walls. We are all aware of the many teacher education courses, professional development opportunities, publications, professional associations, and other resources that are available to us. By making use of them we contribute to a positive atmosphere for education in all contexts.

❶ How do you keep in touch with the profession at large?

- ☐ I read professional newsletters, journals, or other publications.
- ☐ I go to meetings, presentations, and workshops.
- ☐ I hold membership in a professional organisation.
- ☐ I subscribe to or borrow publications from professional organisations.
- ☐ I visit resource centres.
- ☐ Other: _____

❷ Devise an action plan that will help you learn more about your pupils and contribute to your continuing professional development.

Summary

In this chapter the tasks have encouraged you to examine your relationships with your managers, colleagues and pupils. Use your responses to these tasks to consider ways that could improve your relationships with these people in order to improve your professional practice. Copies of your responses to particular tasks and evidence of improvement in that area can be used to inform your professional development record. Evidence of this might be minutes of meetings, extracts from a reflection journal, notes about a conversation or comments you have received from managers, colleagues or pupils about your relationship with them.

Try to picture a classroom from 100 years ago — for example, a room where a language lesson was in progress. Imagine the rows of pupils obediently slouched over their texts, conjugating Latin verbs in unison or translating Greek. If you had asked them to say 'Good-bye' in the language they were learning, they probably would not have been able to. But then, they did not really need to — learning for them was not about being able to communicate their own ideas.

Readers of this book will find no resemblance between this description and their own teaching environments. Today's classrooms are intended to promote enjoyment in learning, to encourage collaboration and interaction, and to help pupils develop real skills they will need in real life. How you organise your physical space and the ethos you create in it contribute to the success of that mission.

Your classroom

Classrooms come in a multitude of colours, shapes, and sizes. Some were designed originally as settings for learning and teaching, with plenty of room and wall space, good ventilation, and good lighting. Quite often, however, instruction takes place in conditions quite removed from that ideal. Classes for adults, particularly, may be held in adapted offices or rooms in community centres or libraries, and in the worst-case scenario, these resemble broom cupboards more than classrooms. Some rooms are shared by many teachers and therefore cannot be claimed by anyone as his own. The result is bare walls and a cold, unfriendly, temporary sort of feeling. Other rooms accommodate oversize classes, and the clutter of furniture allows no possibility of rearranging desks to facilitate student interaction and mobility.

A teacher's wish list of what a classroom should be like would probably include the following:

- spacious and clean;
- lots of whiteboard and wall space;
- good lighting and ventilation;
- ample space for storage of instructional materials;
- windows that open, with sills for plants or displays;
- provision and facilities for ICT;
- large tables (rather than small desks) for group work; and
- good climate control.

We spend so much time in our classrooms that quite often we stop noticing things that a casual visitor would immediately pick up. At one time or another, we have all had books or papers piled in inappropriate places, Christmas decorations still hanging in May, and faded samples of pupils' work or obsolete posters drooping on the walls. The following tasks are intended to help you look at your classroom with fresh eyes.

Task 1

❶ Use the following chart to create an objective account of what a visitor would see upon entering your classroom.

Item	What do you see?
My desk (and things on it)	_____
Pupils' desks	_____
Other furniture	_____
Storage space	_____
Whiteboard	_____
Shelves	_____
Floor	_____
Walls (and things on them)	_____
Other	_____

❷ Identify what you like and dislike about your classroom.

❸ Identify all the things that frustrate you about your classroom.

❹ What would you like to change? Is it within your power to change these things?

❺ If your classroom is far removed from the ideal or if you are not allowed, for example, to rearrange furniture or post things on the walls, how do you make the most of what is available?

❻ If you are not based in one classroom but move from room to room, how do you make the best of this situation?

Task 2

In many cases, you can go a long way towards shaping your teaching environment. Reflect on the appearance of your classroom in general.

❶ What do you do to make your classroom a pleasant, stimulating environment?

	Always				Never
	5	4	3	2	1
I organise classroom space and seating arrangements to facilitate interaction and learning.	☐	☐	☐	☐	☐
I display pupils' work in my room and elsewhere in the school.	☐	☐	☐	☐	☐
I display visual aids for topics currently being explored.	☐	☐	☐	☐	☐
I change classroom displays regularly and keep them neat.	☐	☐	☐	☐	☐
I Involve pupils in decorating the room and keeping it tidy.	☐	☐	☐	☐	☐
Other:_____	☐	☐	☐	☐	☐

❶ In your case, how true is the following statement? 'A visitor to my classroom would probably think that it looks stimulating, clean, and tidy.'

True ☐　　Somewhat true ☐　　Not true ☐

❷ Are there things you could improve? How will you do it?

Task 3

Most teachers are expected to be in class before the start of their lessons, since advance preparation of teaching aids, materials, items on the blackboard, etc., ensures that teaching time is maximised.

❶ What happens in your classroom before and during each class?

	Always				Never
	5	4	3	2	1
The whiteboard is clean before the class starts.	☐	☐	☐	☐	☐
Materials are ready – handouts photocopied, tapes cued, and so on.	☐	☐	☐	☐	☐
My desk is well organised and tidy.	☐	☐	☐	☐	☐
I set a good example by being on time myself.	☐	☐	☐	☐	☐
I discuss with pupils the expectations related to being on time.	☐	☐	☐	☐	☐
I respect break time (everyone needs it).	☐	☐	☐	☐	☐
Other:_____	☐	☐	☐	☐	☐

❷ If an observer were asked to give an overall evaluation of your level of preparation for instructional time, what rating would he or she give?

5	4	3	2	1
Excellent				Poor

❸ What could you improve in this area? What is your action plan for doing so?

Seating arrangement, your presence, and eye contact

The physical classroom space can go a long way to establishing an atmosphere conducive to learning. But once your pupils are in the room and instruction has begun, there are other things that should be kept in mind. Different arrangements of desks promote different kinds of interaction, and the way you address your pupils contributes significantly to the learning environment.

Task 1

Draw a plan of your classroom and label the furniture, door(s), window(s), and board.

1 Look at the seating arrangement depicted in your drawing. Are you content with it?

Yes ☐   No ☐

2 How are your pupils seated?

☐   Individually, at small desks.

☐   In pairs.

☐   Grouped around tables, facing one another.

☐   In a semicircle facing my desk.

☐   In a circle.

☐   In rows.

☐   Other: _____

3 Is the seating arrangement conducive to a variety of grouping possibilities – pair, small-group, or whole-class interaction, along with individual work? Can pupils see and hear one another easily? Can they see the board easily?

4 If you do not have control over classroom seating, is there anything you could do to make the most of the existing arrangement?

5 If the seating arrangements can be changed, what could you do to improve them?

Task 2

Use the picture from the preceding task and mark on it the places you usually stand during class time – for example, 'X1' would indicate where you stand most of the time, 'X2' a place you stand somewhat less often, and so on. (If possible, confirm this through video-recording your class for a few days.)

1 To facilitate communication and keep pupils involved, do you stand at a spot where everyone can see and hear you easily? Sit in different pupils' seats and imagine how you would feel during class if you were those pupils.

2 Are there spots in the classroom where you stand more often than others? If yes, is there any particular reason?

3 Once your pupils start doing an activity, do you circulate? Yes ☐   No ☐

4 Experiment with changing your usual spot(s) in the classroom. What impact does this have on class interaction and dynamics?

5 Devise an action plan for improving this aspect of your teaching practice.

Task 3

Analyse your classroom presence and the way you maintain eye contact. If possible, do this by watching a video-recording of yourself teaching.

❶ Which pupils do you usually look at while talking? Where in the room do these pupils sit?

❷ Do you have any specific reasons for focusing on these pupils and classroom positions? If so, what are they? If not, would you like to alter anything? Do you focus more on boys than girls or vice versa?

❸ Do you tend to look over the pupils' heads? Yes ☐ No ☐

❹ Do you feel that making eye contact benefits pupils? Yes ☐ No ☐

❺ In some cultures it is polite to avert the eyes, do you have any pupils from these cultures in your class? Yes ☐ No ☐

❻ Do you think that all your pupils feel they get a fair share of your attention?

❼ Devise an action plan to improve this aspect of your teaching practice.

Task 4

While doing an activity with the whole class, a teacher asks one pupil to read aloud. As the pupil starts reading, the teacher moves to stand by the pupil's desk, anticipating that he will need help. The pupil begins to read more softly, concentrating on the teacher, with the result that some of his peers now cannot hear him. These pupils, realising that the teacher is busy with this pupil, start talking among themselves. It takes the teacher quite a while to regain control of the class and their attention.

❶ The next time you are working on a whole-class activity and during it ask one pupil to read aloud, do an experiment by filling in this chart.

What do I do?	Insert a tick each time	Why did I do that?
I remain in the same spot.	☐	_____
I move closer.	☐	_____
I stand beside the pupil who is reading.	☐	_____

❷ Do your different actions have different effects? If yes, what are they?

_____

_____

Task 5

One source of frustration in the classroom may be related to an inappropriate number of pupils.

❶ How many pupils do you have in your class (or, on average, in each of your classes)?

❷ Do you feel that the number is appropriate for the space and your obligations? If the number is high, how do you cope?

❸ If you have a new pupil join your class or one of your classes, how do you cope?

☐ Do you help new pupils catch up with the class?

☐ Do you show new pupils your scheme of work, telling them what they have missed and explaining how you might work together to cover this material?

☐ Do you assign a peer mentor to a new pupil?

☐ Do you teach more than one group within your class and assign the new learner to an appropriate group after assessment?

☐ Other:_____

❹ Are you content with the way you are dealing with this situation? If not, what is your action plan?

Whiteboard use and organisation

Task 1

Despite technological advances, a board is still a useful and reliable teaching aid. Even in resource-poor schools, a board is usually available. Reflect on how you use the board by ticking the appropriate column for each statement.

	Always			Never	
I begin with a clean board, if possible.	☐	☐	☐	☐	☐
I write legibly.	☐	☐	☐	☐	☐
I avoid mixing printing and cursive writing or upper- and lower-case letters.	☐	☐	☐	☐	☐
I start writing on the left-hand side.	☐	☐	☐	☐	☐
I keep my writing organised and neat.	☐	☐	☐	☐	☐
I use coloured chalk or board markers.	☐	☐	☐	☐	☐
I erase as often as appropriate.	☐	☐	☐	☐	☐
I keep my back turned to the class for short periods only.	☐	☐	☐	☐	☐
I avoid talking while writing on the board with my back to the class.	☐	☐	☐	☐	☐
When I'm writing on the board, I turn around occasionally and talk about what I'm writing in order to address pupils who are not visually oriented.	☐	☐	☐	☐	☐
I ask pupils if they can read my writing.	☐	☐	☐	☐	☐
I ask pupils whether their perception of what needs to be written on the board matches my practice.	☐	☐	☐	☐	☐
I encourage pupils to write on the board.	☐	☐	☐	☐	☐
Other:_____	☐	☐	☐	☐	☐

Task 2

In her 1993 book *Classroom Observation Tasks* (p. 123), Ruth Wajnryb describes the board as an invaluable classroom resource and suggests the following organisation of space to maximise its effectiveness:

Reference material (permanent)	Main section – developmental stages of lesson	Impromptu notes – 'perishables'

❶ How does this organisation compare with the way you use the board?

❷ Does this organisation, along with what you learned by completing the preceding task, suggest any areas that could be improved? If so, what are they?

❸ Create an action plan for making the improvement(s), and monitor progress for about a week. What happened?

Your role in the classroom

Task 1

Teachers assume a number of different roles, depending on their perceptions, methodology and preferences.

❶ Think of yesterday's lesson. Place a tick next to the descriptors that best fit the roles you took on during its various stages. Then circle the roles that you would *like* to see yourself in.

manager	initiator	motivator	psychologist
controller	lecturer	helper	actor/performer
authority	informer	facilitator	presenter
organiser	explainer	provider of services	assistant
assessor	stimulator	entertainer	consultant

other: _____

❷ Most of the time you see yourself as a …?

❸ You would most like to see yourself as a …?

❹ How can you come to fill the role selected in question 3?

Task 2

In the 1995 article 'Taming the Big "I": Teacher Performance and Student Satisfaction,' Jeremy Harmer discusses results of an interview conducted with a number of teachers from different countries. The primary question was: 'Are you a different person in the classroom from the one you are out of the classroom?' Many teachers replied that in the classroom they felt like performers on stage and that they exhibited more positive characteristics (humour, creativity, etc.) in class than they did in 'real life'.

How would you respond to the same interview question?

Task 3

Successful pupils are usually those capable of organising themselves, keeping their class notes and handouts in order and referring to them on a regular basis. In order to help pupils, our roles can extend beyond delivering input to showing pupils how that input can be managed.

❶ To what extent do you feel that well-organised pupil notes affect their progress?

❷ Do any of your pupils carry their books, handouts and papers in a disorganised, dog-eared pile? Do some of them lose their handouts or leave them behind? Do you think that your role as an organiser, controller, and helper forces you to intervene? If yes, what should you do? If no, why not?

❸ In general, do you feel teachers should encourage pupils to keep well-organised notes and class materials? If so, how?

❹ Do you encourage pupils to take down the date and objective for each lesson and to keep well-organised notes? How much control should the teacher exert in this area?

❺ What factors influence your decisions on this aspect of teaching and learning?

Summary
In this chapter you have considered how to improve the layout of your teaching area(s), how you interact with your class and how you see your role as a teacher. Use copies of the tasks you have completed along with photographs of your classroom or audio-/video-tapes of your teaching to evidence professional development in these areas.

Hay McBer (2000) indicates that an important characteristic of effective teaching is effective preparation. If asked to name three factors essential to successful teaching, many teacher trainers would agree on preparation, preparation, preparation.

Solid preparation takes considerable effort but is important for all teachers, especially newly qualified ones. It involves familiarisation with attainment targets, National Curriculum programmes of study, literacy, numeracy and ICT strategies to create a long-range plan and undertaking reflection on daily lesson plans. It results in a well-designed and well-implemented course, built around goals relevant for a particular group of pupils. Such planning gives teachers and pupils a clear picture of the curriculum content and organisation.

Because it is so time-consuming, preparation is probably the least popular and most burdensome aspect of teaching. At the same time, teachers and teacher trainers (and pupils!) would certainly recognise it as one of the most rewarding. The consolation is that it does become easier as years go by and a teacher's repertoire of techniques and materials grows.

Teaching and learning styles

Although much of the content that we teach is determined by the National Curriculum, programmes of study and the strategies determined by the DfES teachers can ensure that the delivery of this material is matched appropriately to the pupils in their classes. The following tasks will enable you to consider how effectively you match your teaching style with the learning styles of your pupils.

Task 1

❶ We all know that preferences and styles of teaching and learning are extremely varied. Have you checked if the teaching style you use is the style your pupils prefer?

❷ Have you developed a checklist or questionnaire for your pupils related to their learning preferences and styles? Have you discussed these with your pupils? Have you analysed their responses and reactions? Are these reflected in your schemes of work?

❸ Do you feel you have an understanding of what your pupils' needs are? How could you better understand these needs?

Curriculum goals

One of the steps in designing a scheme of work is to define a set of general goals. This will help you clarify and make concrete your thinking about the aims of your teaching. Goals might include:

- assisting pupils in achieving the knowledge, skills and understanding for a particular programme of study;

- helping pupils master a particular subject, skill or content base, e.g. scientific enquiry;
- providing pupils with the means to develop their communicative abilities.

Task 1

❶ How are your general goals defined? Formulate a statement of goals.

❷ How well do these goals relate to the needs of your pupils?

❸ How can you better ensure that your goals relate better to the needs of your pupils?

Curricula and schemes of work

Preparing to teach involves, obviously, knowing the curriculum. Whether you are designing the scheme of work yourself or following a predetermined outline, you will need to consider how it will proceed over the long term.

Task 1

Many teachers do not have the option of designing their own curricula. What circumstances do you work in?

❶ I have to follow a preset curriculum, designed by the DfES, school or department.

Yes ☐   No ☐   Partly ☐   Selectively ☐

If so, how do you feel about the curriculum? Did you have input into designing it? Have you ever provided your line managers with feedback on it?

❷ I have to design a course for each new group of pupils.

Yes ☐   No ☐

If so, do you adapt an established curriculum for each new group? How?

❸ I have to use a syllabus presented in a commercial publication.

Yes ☐   No ☐   Selectively ☐

If so, how do you feel about the syllabus? Have you ever provided your line managers with feedback on it?

Task 2

Preparing your long-term plan may include selecting the order of units and topics to teach, deciding on the amount of time to allot to each of them, setting lessons at the appropriate level, and so on.

❶ Decisions related to your long-term plan are so crucial that they can make or break your teaching. Wrong decisions can lead pupils to develop a negative attitude about your class, thereby undermining learning, or, in the case of adult learners, drive them away in search of a better-planned course. Which decisions do you feel are particularly important? List and rank them below.

Decisions related to...	Essential 5	4	3	2	Less important 1
Order of units/topics	☐	☐	☐	☐	☐
Amount of time allocated	☐	☐	☐	☐	☐
Differentiation in lessons	☐	☐	☐	☐	☐
Teaching style	☐	☐	☐	☐	☐
Learning activities	☐	☐	☐	☐	☐

Task 3

Now look at your long-term plan or scheme of work and determine if you have identified the subject matter, topics, units, structures, skills, and so on that you plan to teach. Have you sequenced the components logically? Do you spiral course content and topics, coming back to review and expand on material previously taught? Have you designed appropriate activities?

❶ If a colleague read your long-term plan, would he or she be able to identify what your pupils will be able to do at the end of your course?

Yes ☐   Partly ☐   No ☐   I don't know ☐

❷ Ask a colleague to read your course outline. Is your response to question 1 correct?

Yes ☐   No ☐

❸ Answer these questions about your long-term planning practice.

In order to develop a solid long-term plan...	Always	Usually	Sometimes	Never
I create a clear and appropriate course outline and make it available to pupils.	☐	☐	☐	☐
I ask for pupils' suggestions on units and topics.	☐	☐	☐	☐
I sequence units and techniques from 'easier' to 'more difficult'.	☐	☐	☐	☐
I take into account the development of all the skills included.	☐	☐	☐	☐
I reflect on and improve my long-term plan over time.	☐	☐	☐	☐
I show sensitivity to the developmental stage of my pupils and to their personal situations.	☐	☐	☐	☐

❹ Based on an analysis of your answers, what areas of planning may require work over the next few weeks? What is your action plan?

Planning for task-based instruction

Your long-term plan will include many aspects of what will be taught, why, when, and how. The 'how' component clearly relates to the overall philosophy of instruction in your teaching. Many curricula today follow a task-based instructional approach – that is, rather than the teacher delivering the course content through lectures and traditional assignments, pupils pursue learning through a series of hands-on activities. By opting for such an approach, teachers can ensure that their pupils are equipped with the skills they will need outside the classroom.

Task 1

The following are some features that might be found in a task-based teaching course. Read the list and tick the items that apply to your curricula. Does or will it include:

- clear instructional goals;
- authentic/naturalistic data;
- cooperative group tasks;
- linked sequences of tasks;
- models/examples of what is expected;
- individual tasks;
- opportunities for learners to make choices;
- opportunities for pupils to contribute their own ideas, opinions and feelings;
- opportunities for pupils to self-check and self-assess;
- outside-class application opportunities.

Task 2

When designing tasks to be carried out in the classroom, it is important to keep in mind pupils' lives outside the classroom. By doing this we can ensure that our task-based activities provide pupils with the language, skills and knowledge that they need for their lives outside the classroom.

There is a difference between *pedagogic tasks* and *authentic tasks*. The former will usually ask pupils to do something they would not normally be asked to do outside a classroom, e.g. answer questions from a reading or decide which statements are true or false. Some of these activities are of course necessary, but they will be most effective if they have clear links to life outside the classroom. Authentic tasks engage pupils in activities they might encounter in their life outside the classroom, e.g. listening to a radio talk show and deciding whether they agree or disagree with a caller. Although pedagogic and authentic tasks cannot always be clearly distinguished, it is important for teachers to incorporate both in their planning.

❶ Examine some recent lesson plans, identify the tasks they include, and then fill in the chart below. The first row gives an example.

Pedagogic tasks	Authentic tasks
1. To develop listening comprehension, pupils listen to a tape-recorded traffic report and place ticks next to statements about it that are true.	1. Pupils receive a list of locations mentioned in a tape-recorded traffic report. Prior to listening, they select a location where they will be 'driving.' During playback of the tape, they determine whether their location is affected by adverse traffic conditions and decide how this might affect their chosen route.
2. _____	2. _____
3. _____	3. _____
4. _____	4. _____

Task 3

Select and evaluate one of the tasks you expected pupils to perform in the past few days. Consider first whether it was pedagogic or authentic, and then complete the following chart.

	Very much so			Not at all	
	5	4	3	2	1
The task was set at the appropriate level for all or most pupils. (If not, think about how it could be modified.)	☐	☐	☐	☐	☐
The task was interesting and motivating enough to keep pupils involved.	☐	☐	☐	☐	☐
I structured the task to involve authentic types of communication.	☐	☐	☐	☐	☐
The task was based on pupils sharing information, which thereby created a real need for cooperation and communication.	☐	☐	☐	☐	☐
I designed the task differently from others used on that day or during that week, to provide variety.	☐	☐	☐	☐	☐
It was designed to prepare pupils for vital tasks in the world outside the classroom.	☐	☐	☐	☐	☐

Task 4

In many instructional settings, teachers must follow a prescribed curriculum in which pedagogic tasks are emphasised. If this is your situation, there are still things you can do to ensure that the pedagogic tasks you must use are meaningful.

❶ List several common tasks in your course and evaluate the degree to which they assist pupils in achieving overall goals.

Task: _____

5	4	3	2	1
Very helpful			Could be more helpful	

Task: _____

5	4	3	2	1
Very helpful			Could be more helpful	

Task: _____

5	4	3	2	1
Very helpful			Could be more helpful	

❷ How could you modify those tasks you rated at the bottom of the scale so that they would draw connections to authentic needs and interests?

Summary

In this chapter you have considered how you design your schemes of work and long-term plans that are needed to deliver the National Curriculum programmes of study. You have also considered the type of tasks you incorporate in these plans and whether they are pedagogic or authentic. Use copies of your answers to the tasks along with revised or completed schemes of work and plans and pieces of pupil work as evidence of continuing professional development. These can be used to make up your professional development record.

Lesson plans are the tools we use to reflect on content, context, techniques, materials, sequencing and timing, and a variety of other aspects of curriculum design. They allow us to maintain the high quality of our teaching. The differences between a well-planned and an unplanned lesson are comparable to those between a movie with a script and one without. If they don't know their lines, the actors may end up shooting the good guys instead of the bad. The consequences in the classroom are not so drastic, but they definitely have a negative impact on the quality of learning and teaching.

Expectations related to daily planning vary considerably from school to school and department to department. In some contexts, teachers are expected to have long-term and daily plans and to submit them to line managers. In others, planning is left totally to the teacher's discretion. But regardless of whether lesson planning is supervised or not, we must still think of it as a requirement. Lessons simply cannot be meaningful if they are not thoroughly prepared. Well-planned lessons flow smoothly, building on what has happened before, leading to what will happen next, and with components and segments seeming just to fall into place. They are clear, logical, easy to carry out, and – perhaps most important – they are constructed to work for your particular pupils. Everyone who has seen a well-planned lesson unfold would admit that it was a pleasure to observe and participate in. Of course, we have all entered our classrooms under-prepared on occasion, and have put lessons together as we went along. Sometimes, for example, we might have a list of activities to be undertaken but no clearly defined framework for connecting them; at worst, we may have only a vague idea of what to do during the lesson. Pupils are astute consumers of services, and they can tell when their teacher is unprepared. Observing an improvised lesson is like watching a disaster unfold: there are all kinds of unplanned events, behaviour problems, activities that drag on, and discussions that lead nowhere.

One way of highlighting for yourself the difference between a prepared and an unprepared lesson is to do the following experiment. The next time you, for whatever reason, have to teach a lesson without much (if any) preparation, write a lesson plan *after* the session, and compare this plan of what could have been done to what actually happened. An even more objective procedure is to video-tape an unplanned lesson and then to analyse what went on and consider how certain events could have been avoided by planning.

The essential role of lesson planning is beyond debate. We are in a powerful position in the classroom, and we have to bear in mind that the fate of the course often depends on how thoroughly prepared we are. In this chapter teachers have the opportunity to analyse their planning practice and re-evaluate their beliefs, habits, preconceptions, and procedures.

Unit planning/topics

Lessons are not isolated entities but are part of a larger, longer context. Whether that context is called a unit, theme, or some other name, it indicates a sequence of lessons connected by general objectives and topic. The first step in lesson planning, then, could be thought of as unit planning. This usually involves applying a common-sense approach to selecting and sequencing components.

Imagine that you are a teacher whose curriculum includes study of health issues. You might begin your planning by identifying health-related topics that students need to study e.g. nutrition, exercise, drugs, disease etc.

After deciding on lesson topics you would analyse the general objectives for the unit, consider the tasks pupils have to perform outside the classroom and refer to the National Curriculum programmes of study for the specific skills and concepts that need to be taught.

Task 1

Do you plan around units or topics? If so, analyse two of them.

❶ How do they correspond to the needs of your pupils?

❷ How do lessons reflect authentic situations your pupils will face?

❸ How do particular components of your units and the skills and knowledge they aim to teach reflect the general objectives?

❹ How well are the lessons within your unit linked so that they build on and reinforce one another? How could you improve this aspect of the unit?

Designing a lesson plan

No lesson plan will work equally well for all groups of pupils. Our purpose with this section, therefore, is not to prescribe a format for lesson planning but to walk through an example of the process in order to outline the important factors and some common errors.

Lesson plans can take many different forms and include a wide variety of content. The lesson planning process that follows illustrates a simple, generalised version of the sort of plan that could be created to achieve the described objectives. Individual teachers could add more versatility or more local context to the planning, develop new activities, or rely more on published materials. If you are a newly qualified teacher, read this section to get an idea of possible routes on the lesson-planning journey and the choices you might face along the way. Experienced teachers may choose to compare the plan outlined here with their own model, in order to focus reflection and identify areas for improvement.

Imagine the following situation. Lara teaches science to a mixed-ability Year-7 class. The next unit she is planning to teach is related to the health topic. What process does Lara go through when planning a lesson?

The initial assessment: asking 'what' questions

Lara's first step in creating a lesson plan is to determine the content that needs to be taught. Lara refers to the National Curriculum programme of study for science and identifies that the pupils should be taught that the abuse of alcohol, solvents and other drugs affects health. In addition to this she intends to incorporate elements of the literacy strategy and ICT in the lesson as well as developing research skills.

The first part of Lara's lesson plan might look like this:

Date:	January 18
Duration:	60 minutes
Unit:	Health
Topic:	Alcohol abuse
Objectives:	1. Pupils will be able to carry out research about alcohol.
	2. Pupils will explain the effects of alcohol abuse.
	3. Pupils will use ICT to report their findings.

One of the most common traps of the lesson-planning process would be to brainstorm a list of activities and materials that could be used without considering seriously the desired objectives. The result is usually a mismatch between activities and objectives. Although starting the process by listing activities is by no means an incorrect method, teachers who decide to do this need to be careful not to lose touch with lesson and unit objectives.

With the objectives defined, Lara can now ask herself, 'What will my pupils need to know and do in order to achieve the objective I have identified?' The lesson plan can now be extended to include the following:

Skills:	Research and cooperative skills, clarity of written communication, use of ICT.
Concepts:	Alcohol is a drug. Alcohol is a legal drug which is easily available but which can cause serious health problems. Alcohol affects the brain and the nervous system, it is a depressant. Alcohol can be addictive. Alcohol affects people's judgment. Drinking large amounts of alcohol over a number of years can lead to stomach ulcers, heart disease, cirrhosis of the liver and brain damage.
Vocabulary:	Alcohol, drug, addict, depressant.

Options for answering the 'how to' questions

Once the what-to-teach questions have been answered, the relevant question becomes how to teach the content. Generally the sequence of the lesson should follow the natural sequence of learning. Some teachers will recognise this as the 'three Ps' approach of presentation, practice, and production; others will recognise this as *precommunicative practice* followed by *communicative practice*. First the new knowledge, skills, topic, information – or whatever the 'what' of the lesson – is presented or taught. Then learners are given a chance to try things out, make mistakes, receive feedback, be corrected, and try again. Finally, they have opportunities to use the newly learned concepts on their own.

For Lara, the first choice is between two broad possibilities for introducing new content. Her decision will depend on learner preferences, expectations, and learning and teaching styles, and it will feed into her decisions about the nature and sequencing of the lesson's other activities. Both approaches have strengths and weaknesses, and they should both be part of the teacher's repertoire, in order to provide balance and avoid dull routine.

In a *deductive presentation*, movement is from the larger context to the building blocks. This is a discovery technique, and in Lara's teaching context it might involve research activities that would involve pupils using leaflets, the internet, books and magazines to find information on alcohol and its effects. This type of introduction would be followed by activities designed to focus their knowledge, learn how to use it and finally culminate in a communicative task to summarise what they have learnt.

An *inductive presentation* starts with the building blocks. For Lara, this would mean introducing the main concepts and vocabulary, followed by practice activities and finally a task such as a role-play to bring the concepts together.

Lara's lesson plan may now include a description of the procedures she intends to use:

1. *Review:*	Review last lesson and homework. Introduce the topic.
2. *Introduction:*	Ask what the pupils already know about alcohol and its effects on the body, brainstorm their ideas on the whiteboard, discuss vocabulary and concepts.
3. *Practice:*	Small groups research resource materials for additional information about alcohol and its effects and make notes.
4. *Production:*	Whole class adds to initial brainstorm with additional information. Then each individual produces leaflet or magazine article using ICT about alcohol and its effects.
5. *Review:*	Move around the class to discuss individual work.

Evaluation: asking why

The last stage of designing a lesson plan is to evaluate the activities against the intended objectives and desired outcomes. A well-planned lesson is not a motley collection of activities but a sequence organised for a purpose.

Task 1

❶ Analyse Lara's lesson plan. Are the objectives achievable through the set of activities outlined?

Yes ☐   No ☐   To some extent ☐

❷ Do each of the activities play a part in achieving the overall objectives? If yes, how? If no, why not?

❸ How does this lesson plan relate to your teaching circumstances? Would something similar be feasible with your pupils? What might hinder its realisation in your class(es)? What, if anything, would you like to change in it?

❹ How does Lara's lesson planning process differ from your own?

Task 2

A group of pupils is leaving the classroom after a lesson. A visitor stops them and asks, 'What did you study today?' 'English,' they respond unanimously after an awkward pause.

Think about your pupils. Would they be able to provide a more specific answer in the same situation? Find out by asking your pupils this same question.

Lesson objectives

Objectives state what pupils will be able to do at the end of the lesson and reflect the extent to which we expect that teaching will result in learning. Defining objectives well – and, above all, accomplishing them – is one of our essential tasks.

When working on planning, teachers usually pay more attention to a lesson's content, activities, and stages than to assessing how each lesson segment fits into objectives. But determining what pupils will be able to do as a result of instruction deserves as much attention as identifying what will be taught and how.

Task 1

Reflect on the importance of objectives in your lesson plans.

❶ How important do you feel defining objectives is in the lesson-planning process?

5   4   3   2   1

Very important   Not important

❷ Do you feel you devote enough time to defining objectives?

Yes ☐   No ☐   Probably ☐

❸ When you finish writing your lesson plans, do you go back to check whether the activities you selected will actually help pupils accomplish the identified objectives?

Yes ☐   No ☐

❹ What do you do if the objectives and the activities do not match?

☐ I redefine the objectives.

☐ I change or adjust the activities.

☐ Other: _____

❺ If objectives are intended to describe the result of classroom instruction, then well-formulated objectives should be specific and expressed in terms of observable and measurable behaviours. Such a formulation might state that pupils will be able to 'list', 'compare and contrast', 'report', 'explain', or 'describe', rather than 'know', 'understand,' or 'learn.' Further, objectives should not describe what pupils will be doing during the actual lesson (e.g. 'read a story,' 'study the vocabulary') but rather what they will be able to do as a result of your instruction. Read the following examples of objectives and reflect on how their formulation differs from yours.

- Pupils will be able to write about a past event.
- Pupils will be able to draw the position of major organs in the body.
- Pupils will be able to complete a timeline of significant events in history.
- Pupils will be able to identify lines of symmetry.

6 Leaf through your lesson plans and make a list of the verbs you use to define objectives. Do they all express 'observable', 'measurable' behaviours?

Task 2

Analyse the way in which your objectives are worded.

1 Are they clear and understandable?

Yes ☐   No ☐   Almost ☐

2 Do they define what pupils will be able to do at the end of – rather than during – the lesson?

Yes ☐   No ☐   Almost ☐

3 Are there sufficient objectives for each lesson?

Yes ☐   No ☐   Almost ☐

4 Do you manage to accomplish the objectives without rushing?

Yes ☐   No ☐   Almost ☐

5 Do you provide sufficient opportunity for practice before expecting pupils to attain each objective?

Yes ☐   No ☐   Almost ☐

Task 3

Good lesson planning is not easy. Potential problem areas related to objectives include:

- lack of a clear definition;
- defining the objectives well, but overlooking them during the lesson so that things take an unexpected turn in the classroom;
- existence of a mismatch between pupils' and teacher's perceptions of the objectives;
- existence of a conflict between pupils' and teacher's perceptions of the objectives.

In general, difficulties related to defining objectives, organising lessons so that they can be achieved, and explaining them to pupils diminish with experience. Beginning teachers may devote more time to the 'what' and 'how' elements of the lesson than to the 'why.' To avoid such difficulties, try the following task.

❶ Before three of your next lessons, fill out the objectives column in the following chart. At the end of each lesson, ask your pupils for feedback on what they thought the objectives of the day were. (Make sure your pupils understand the word *objectives*.) Now complete the chart. What conclusions can you draw?

	The objectives I set	What pupils thought the objectives were	Digressions I made in class: Why? Were they justified?
Lesson 1	_____	_____	_____
Lesson 2	_____	_____	_____
Lesson 3	_____	_____	_____

❷ Is there considerable difference between the objectives you set and those perceived by your pupils? If so, devise an action plan to address this issue.

Transitions

A well-planned lesson has clearly defined stages with smooth transitions from one to the next. Its framework might look like this:

Clearly signalled beginning

Statement of objectives

Explanation of lesson procedures and activities

Body (segments each with a clear purpose, linked sequentially and to the objectives)

Conclusion (summary, clearly signalled ending)

Task 1

Analyse the framework of a recent lesson plan against the one above.

❶ How did you start your lesson?

❷ How many lesson stages can you identify?

❸ How were the stages related to one another?

❹ How were they related to the objectives?

❺ How did you signal transitions from one stage to the next?

❻ Was there a logical connection between the stages?

❼ How did you end the lesson?

❽ What can you conclude?

Task 2

Before you teach your next lesson, identify at least two of its stages and think about what you are going to say or do to link them.

The stages   **The transition**

1. _____   _____

2. _____   _____

Others: _____   _____

After the lesson, think about whether the planned transition worked out well.

Variety

Have you ever tried to identify the ingredients of an uninteresting lesson? The list would probably include repetition of the same sorts of activities in the same order, reusing the same resources, and lack of variety in topics. A common misconception among teachers is that using the same format and approach for every lesson is beneficial. Teachers sometimes say that this is what their pupils want, that they appreciate the familiar structure. There is, indeed, something to be said for the comfort that comes from familiar routines: the pupils feel informed, they prepare themselves for particular activities, and any confusion about new content is not compounded by confusion about lesson procedures. However, there is a clear line between familiarity and monotony. It is the same line that distinguishes excellence from mediocrity, creativity from dullness, sensitivity from the lack of it. Simply put, too much of any routine leads to boredom, a major classroom enemy that results in dissatisfaction, lower motivation, and profound negative effects on teaching and learning.

This is not to say that we must be wildly creative and dynamic all the time. We all remember teachers who did not bring much variety, creativity, or fun into their classes, but were still well liked and respected. Such teachers know that a teaching-matches-learning formula can make up for a certain lack of fun. But regardless of your style, hard work is required to bring the right balance of routine, variety, and excitement to your classroom.

Task 1

Think about the routines you use in teaching and the variety you build into your lessons.

❶ Do you tend to use the same or similar layouts for lessons each day? Why or why not?

❷ If you do tend to revisit the same routines, how do you avoid monotony and boredom?

❸ Try an experiment. Teach a lesson using a different approach and change your routine. Involve your pupils – explain to them what you want to do and why, and collect feedback from them. What happened?

Localising and personalising the context and content

Learning is enhanced when content and context are personalised and localised. Language learners, for example, often discover that 'attaching' new vocabulary, phrases, or idioms to themselves and their own lives helps make the new language more meaningful, and therefore easier to learn and retain. Teachers should therefore avoid 'clinical,' dry, decontextualized content; instead, lessons should be related to people, places, and things in the pupils' daily experience.

Task 1

Analyse your last two lesson plans and respond to the questions below.

❶ How did you bring your pupils' personal experiences into the content of the lesson?

Lesson 1: _____

_____

Lesson 2: _____

_____

❷ What current events did you draw on (if this is relevant in your teaching circumstances)?

Lesson 1: _____

_____

Lesson 2: _____

_____

❸ What local issues, places or people did you include or refer to (if this is relevant in your teaching curcumstances)?

Lesson 1: _____

_____

Lesson 2: _____

_____

Keeping pupils informed

❶ Do you feel it is important to inform pupils at the beginning of each lesson about what you plan to do and what objectives you have set? Why or why not?

❷ Does informing pupils about plans for the next day or few days work as a motivator? Why or why not?

❸ Monitor how you keep your pupils informed by completing the following chart. For one week of teaching, place a tick under the days when you do the things described.

	Monday	Tuesday	Wednesday	Thursday	Friday
I explained clearly to my pupils what I planned to do during the lesson.					
I explained to my pupils the objectives of the lesson.					
I informed my pupils at the end of the lesson about the plans for the next lesson.					

❹ How do your pupils feel? Make them more involved in their learning by asking them to rate the importance they attach to being informed.

5　　　4　　　3　　　2　　　1

Very important　　　　　　　　Not important

❺ Do you write an outline of the lesson on the board before each lesson? Why or why not? Have you asked your pupils if they would appreciate such an outline?

Reflective lesson plans

A lesson plan is first and foremost a tool. It helps us keep lessons on track from the objectives to their accomplishment. But regardless of how well prepared we might be, lessons often do not proceed according to plan. As the classroom events unfold, an observant teacher might realise that things are not following the script, and adaptations and digressions might be made on the spur of the moment.

Truly effective lesson plans include notes about any changes, jotted down during the lesson for later consideration. 'Went well,' 'Too challenging,' 'Took much more time than planned,' 'Do this after the explanation phase,' and so on testify to the fact that planning is ongoing. Such notes promote reflection about teaching practice and guide us as we develop plans for future lessons.

Task 1

❶ Annotate you lesson plan with notes for one lesson. Was it useful? In what ways?

❷ At the end of each teaching day, set aside ten minutes for personal reflection. Jot down your thoughts. How do you feel the day went? Did everything fall into place? If not, what could have been done differently?

Planning homework

Daily homework gives pupils additional time for learning. However, the approach to homework differs considerably across schools and departments: some include it as a regular part of curriculum, while in others, for a wide variety of reasons, it may be totally absent.

Task 1

Consider the questions below and determine a plan of action that will ensure homework assignments that you set are carefully designed to benefit pupils.

❶ Is homework part of your curriculum? If not, why?

❷ What do you see as the purpose of homework assignments?

❸ Do your pupils want homework assignments? Do they enjoy them and consider them necessary?

Yes ☐   To some extent ☐   No ☐   I don't know ☐

❹ If homework is a part of your curriculum, how often do you set it?

Daily ☐   Every other day ☐   Twice a week ☐   Once a week ☐

❺ How much time do you spend planning homework assignments?

❻ Do you mark pupils' homework? Why or why not? If assignments are marked, how do you go about it?

❼ What types of homework and assignments do you give?

worksheet-type exercises   presentations   other
puzzles and games   out-of-class (community) tasks
guided writing   questions to answer
free writing   research

❾ What, if anything, is your pupils' favourite type of homework?

Task 2

Analyse your last homework assignment.

❶ What was your objective in assigning the task?

❷ Did pupils have sufficient knowledge and adequate strategies to complete the homework? If not, did you help them in a lesson preceding the assignment?

❸ How did the homework help them improve their skills?

❹ Based on your responses to the questions above, how would you rate this particular assignment?

5   4   3   2   1

Excellent   Poor

❺ If you rated the assignment at the low end of the scale, how could you change it for a future group of pupils?

❻ Is there room for improvement in this area? If yes, what is your action plan?

Overall evaluation of daily lessons

Looking back at your lesson plans is one way of improving your planning process. It will also help you ensure that you are covering the course outline as a whole.

Task 1

Reflect on your daily plans for the last week.

	Always	Usually	Sometimes	Never
I planned around the intended objective.				
I planned challenging, but not overwhelming, tasks.				
I included a variety of teaching strategies to address different learning styles and provide variety.				
I referred to my plan during the lessons.				
I noted changes made during the lessons.				

Task 2

Now look more closely at your last three lesson plans.

❶ Is the objective of each lesson clearly stipulated in terms of what pupils will be able to do at its conclusion?

Yes ☐   No ☐

❷ Do your lessons follow a clear, logical framework?

Yes ☐   No ☐

❸ Do the activities lead from the statement of an objective to its achievement?

Yes ☐   No ☐

❹ Are the activities well sequenced?

Yes ☐   No ☐

⑤ Do you use a variety of material relevant to your pupils?

Yes ☐   No ☐

⑥ Were pupils provided with opportunities for practice of new skills and knowledge?

Yes ☐   No ☐

⑦ Did you ask yourself at the end of each lesson how well the objectives had been accomplished?

Yes ☐   No ☐

⑧ How true of your last three lesson plans is the following statement: 'My lesson plans are so clear that a visitor to my class could identify exactly what has been taught and how by analysing them.'

Task 3

This task refers to the evaluation of a single lesson. It can be undertaken as often as you wish, preferably immediately or shortly after the lesson.

❶ Rate how well prepared you were for the lesson. Circle your choice.

Very well   Reasonably well   Not well enough   Minimally

❷ Did the lesson flow as you planned?

❸ Which parts of the lesson were most successful? Why?

❹ Which parts of the lesson were least successful? Why?

❺ What kind of teacher–pupil interaction occurred? How did you ensure that the pupils were actively involved?

❻ How did you respond to individual needs?

❼ How did you gain feedback from your pupils on the lesson?

❽ What did you like about the lesson?

❾ What do you think could have been done better?

❿ Did you depart from your lesson plan? If so, did the change improve the lesson? How?

⓫ How would you teach this lesson differently next time?

⓬ How do you think it would have affected learning if the lesson had been taught differently?

⓮ How do you think pupils felt about this lesson? Did you notice any signals during the lesson that indicated how they felt?

⓯ What do you think an observer would think about this lesson?

Task 4

❶ Analyse the timing of your last lesson.

	Yes				No
	5	4	3	2	1
I accomplished the objectives within the determined time frame.					
I finished all the planned activities. (If not, did you still accomplish the objectives?)					
Some pupils finished activities well ahead of others. (If so, how well did you deal with that?)					
I responded effectively to different pupils' needs in terms of timing.					

❷ Is there room for improvement? If so, what is your action plan?

Summary

In this chapter you have examined possible ways to plan units and lessons and reflected on the way you already do this. You have considered the format of your lessons and the variety of teaching and learning strategies you already use or might use in future. You have reflected on a number of your lessons and have considered how they might be improved. Copies of your responses to these tasks along with annotated lesson plans, pupil and colleague comments and audio- or video-tapes of lessons can be used in your professional development record as evidence of your continuing professional development in the area of lesson planning.

In resource-rich schools teachers have at their disposal a wide array of commercial textbooks, pupil workbooks, teacher reference material, audio and video aids, and an abundance of authentic materials such as magazines, newspapers, brochures and web-sites. Teachers and pupils may also have access to computers at school or at home. Word-processing allows teachers to create their own, very professional and easily adaptable teaching materials, and there are numerous instructional software packages and helpful sites on the Internet that can be utilised as a resource.

In contrast, in some schools the only available teaching tool is the whiteboard, perhaps coupled with one or two copies of a textbook. Practitioners who teach or have taught in the Third World are prepared to find a heart-breaking lack of resources, but even in the 'developed' world supplies vary considerably from school to school. In these settings, teachers' imaginations certainly become the most important resource of all.

Regardless of what resources are available, creativity and resourcefulness seem to be among the most useful qualities teachers can possess. Even in courses that rely on a single textbook, we must use knowledge of the theory and practice of learning and teaching, understanding of our particular pupils, and creativity to provide the best possible learning experience. The security provided by a single text, with its ready-made lesson plans and familiar activities, soon gives way to boredom and reduced learning if it is not supplemented with other materials. Making the most of what we have available and using it with enthusiasm is the rule of thumb in any teaching environment.

Variety

Most teachers strive to select a wide range of resources from which their pupils can benefit. The competitive edge definitely belongs to those who are willing to experiment with an assortment of material and bring variety into their lessons.

Task 1

Look through the selection of resources available for use in your lessons.

❶ Where do you look for resources? Rank order the possibilities on the list below.

☐ They are available on site.

☐ I adapt and expand on the available resources.

☐ I borrow resources from a professional resource centre.

☐ I borrow resources from the local public library.

☐ I buy my own resources.

☐ I create my own resources.

☐ I find resources on the Internet.

☐ I bring authentic materials to the classroom.

☐ I involve pupils in preparation of resources.

☐ Other: _____

❷ How often and in what ways do you use the materials and resources listed in the following chart?

	Daily	Occasionally	Never	Only for my own reference	As a source for adaptation
Curriculum guidelines	☐	☐	☐	☐	☐
Commercial textbooks and workbooks	☐	☐	☐	☐	☐
Teacher's manuals	☐	☐	☐	☐	☐
Authentic materials	☐	☐	☐	☐	☐
Teacher-made materials	☐	☐	☐	☐	☐
Student-made materials	☐	☐	☐	☐	☐
Visual aids	☐	☐	☐	☐	☐
Audio aids	☐	☐	☐	☐	☐
TV and video	☐	☐	☐	☐	☐
Computer software	☐	☐	☐	☐	☐
Internet	☐	☐	☐	☐	☐
Guest speakers	☐	☐	☐	☐	☐
Field trips	☐	☐	☐	☐	☐
Other: _____	☐	☐	☐	☐	☐

❸ Are there some options listed in the preceding questions that you have not used? Why?

❹ Are your resources limited? If so, reflect on the reasons, list sources of frustration, and try to think of some solutions.

Characteristics of resources

The past few decades have witnessed a proliferation of commercial teaching and learning resources. While most new publications adhere to current thinking about teaching methodology, not all are appropriate for every group of learners. Further, we must remember that pupils commonly have a great deal of respect for the printed word, and they trust that everything their teachers bring to the classroom is reliable and correct. It is important that we ensure that our pupils' trust is not misplaced by reviewing and assessing the materials we use, becoming familiar with their limitations, and ensuring that additional material is available to compensate for weaknesses.

Task 1

This task may help you evaluate the texts you are currently using.

❶ Evaluate the resources you use according to the criteria provided.

	Very much			Very little		
Main text	5	4	3	2	1	N/A
The material promotes critical and logical thinking.	☐	☐	☐	☐	☐	☐
The material reinforces the use of a variety of skills and learning strategies.	☐	☐	☐	☐	☐	☐
The text explores all relevant areas of the subject matter.	☐	☐	☐	☐	☐	☐
The text builds on and expands pupils' knowledge of the subject matter.	☐	☐	☐	☐	☐	☐
The material follows a task-based approach.	☐	☐	☐	☐	☐	☐
The material has clear and appropriate goals.						
The material and any included tasks prepare learners for activities and challenges they may face outside the classroom.	☐	☐	☐	☐	☐	☐
Contents are organised into themes and topics.	☐	☐	☐	☐	☐	☐
A variety of text selections that generate interaction, discussion, or learner response are included.	☐	☐	☐	☐	☐	☐
Chapters are of an appropriate length.	☐	☐	☐	☐	☐	☐
The language is clear, authentic (as opposed to simplified or 'bookish') and appropriate for the pupils' level.	☐	☐	☐	☐	☐	☐
The material is appropriate for the learners' age.	☐	☐	☐	☐	☐	☐
Background information is included, where necessary.						
Illustrations and examples are included wherever necessary and are appropriate.	☐	☐	☐	☐	☐	☐
The material can be easily adapted the suit learners' needs and abilities.	☐	☐	☐	☐	☐	☐
The material is culturally sensitive and unbiased.	☐	☐	☐	☐	☐	☐
The material is interesting and enjoyable.	☐	☐	☐	☐	☐	☐

Worksheets

	5	4	3	2	1	N/A
The content of the worksheets has a clear relationship to that of the textbook.	☐	☐	☐	☐	☐	☐
The exercises adequately reinforce and extend the material presented in the main text.	☐	☐	☐	☐	☐	☐
The exercises are meaningful, and provide additional practice for pupils.	☐	☐	☐	☐	☐	☐
The worksheet contains fun activities (e.g., puzzles, wordsearches, games).	☐	☐	☐	☐	☐	☐
An answer key is included.	☐	☐	☐	☐	☐	N/A

Teacher's guide

	5	4	3	2	1	N/A
The teacher's guide clearly identifies the objectives for each unit.	☐	☐	☐	☐	☐	☐
Essential background information is provided for each activity.	☐	☐	☐	☐	☐	☐
An abundance of extension or follow-up ideas (e.g., games, quizzes, exercises) is included.	☐	☐	☐	☐	☐	☐

❷ What conclusions can you draw from your evaluation? What are the elements in the resource you use that make them suitable for your current pupils?

Task 2

Analyse the resources you use in terms of possible bias; their portrayals of different cultural, ethnic, religious, and racial groups; and their depiction of a wide range of people.

The material presents a variety of attitudes and opinions objectively and without prejudice.	Yes ☐	No ☐
The material presents different cultural, ethnic, and religious groups with respect.	Yes ☐	No ☐
Any characters used or people described are not presented as stereotypes.	Yes ☐	No ☐
The illustrations present individuals from a variety of backgrounds and cultures.	Yes ☐	No ☐
No particular lifestyles are promoted over others.	Yes ☐	No ☐
The relationships among people depicted are based on equality and mutual respect.	Yes ☐	No ☐
Women are presented in a variety of roles.	Yes ☐	No ☐
The disabled and the elderly are represented with respect.	Yes ☐	No ☐
Judgmental language (e.g., *primitive, lazy*) is avoided.	Yes ☐	No ☐

Task 3

❶ How often do you ask your pupils' opinion of the resources you use?

❷ What aspects of the resources do pupils comment on?

	Usually	Often	Sometimes	Hardly ever	Never
Topic appropriateness	☐	☐	☐	☐	☐
Level of difficulty	☐	☐	☐	☐	☐
Appearance	☐	☐	☐	☐	☐
Format and layout	☐	☐	☐	☐	☐
Content	☐	☐	☐	☐	☐
Length	☐	☐	☐	☐	☐
Other: _____	☐	☐	☐	☐	☐

❸ Together with a colleague, select a textbook or other resource that you both use and discuss it in terms of the points raised in the questionnaire in Task 1 (p. 44). Do your opinions about the resource differ? If so, how?

④ Design a pupil questionnaire about the resource, using relevant points from the questionnaire in Task 1. What are the results?

Textbooks versus authentic materials

'Authentic' materials are resources we use every day that were not prepared originally for the purposes of instruction. In the language classroom, such materials might include newspapers, magazines, forms or brochures written in the target language. In the primary classroom, a teacher might choose to supplement a commercial reading course with 'real' children's books chosen from the library. In the history classroom, the teacher might introduce genuine artefacts from the period.

Task 1

① From which of these materials do you feel your pupils benefit most? Rank them from 1 to 3.

Authentic materials   Commercial materials   Teacher-developed materials

② Of all the materials you used last week, what percentage fell within each of the three categories?

Authentic materials __ %   Commercial materials __ % Teacher-developed materials __ %

③ Compare the ratings from question 1 with the percentages in question 2. Do you provide a good balance of materials?

Authentic reading materials: newspapers and magazines

What other teaching resource is more up to date and offers something of interest to more people than newspapers and magazines? In addition, these authentic materials are inexpensive, practical, and, if used effectively, popular with pupils. At the same time, these materials are easy to misuse.

To ensure that the newspaper and magazine tasks we assign are at the appropriate level, we should ensure that we design a variety of activities, so that using this medium does not result in boredom. Newspapers and magazines lend themselves well to activities that focus on skills of skimming, scanning, or detailed reading, and strategies such as guessing, predicting, and making inferences. And, of course, they are also useful sources of information in a broad range of disciplines.

Task 1

① How often do you make use of newspapers and magazines in your classroom? Circle one.

quite often   occasionally   rarely   never

② Browse through a newspaper, identify articles you could use with your pupils, and create activities based on them. Possibilities might include a vocabulary search or puzzle, one group creating true–false statements for another group to answer, individual writing of alternate headlines or photo captions, or group staging of a press conference or debate related to a controversial issue.

Describe the activity or activities you devise. What makes them particularly useful and meaningful for your pupils?

Distribution

Decisions about how to distribute materials to pupils do not have a major impact on the quality of teaching. Nevertheless, as with many 'micro' skills, this area deserves some attention since it affects the flow of the lesson.

Task 1

❶ Think about your usual manner of distributing handouts, worksheets or books to your pupils and the rationale behind it. (If you can, video-tape a few lessons and analyse objectively what you do.) Now respond to these statements, indicating what percentage of the time you do the following things.

I give out materials along with instructions to each pupil individually. ____%

I walk around the classroom and give out materials to each pupil individually. ____%

I give a stack of materials to a few pupils at different ends of the room,
saying 'Take one and pass the rest on.' ____%

I pile materials on my desk and ask pupils to come up individually to pick them up. ____%

I ask for volunteers to distribute materials to the rest of the class. ____%

Other:_____ ____%

❷ What is your rationale for the option you use most frequently?

❸ When do you distribute handouts or worksheets for a particular activity?

☐ Before I introduce the activity, because I want pupils to look at them while I give any explanations.

☐ As I begin my introduction and explanations, to save time.

☐ After I introduce the activity, so the pupils will not be distracted from the explanations.

☐ Other:

❹ What is your rationale for selecting the option you use most often?

❺ Monitor this area during a few lessons and experiment with different ways of managing distribution of materials. Have you noticed any problems with any of the approaches? Do you find that one is more effective than others?

Technology in the classroom

Technology has become a part of the classroom furniture. It all started with slide projectors, film strips, overhead projectors, and reel-to-reel movies, and today it has so infiltrated education that it has changed the ways pupils learn and teachers teach. Gone is the traditional pattern established by textbook, teacher, and board; welcome to technology- and computer-assisted learning.

Task 1

1 What technology do you use regularly in your classroom?

slide projector	interactive whiteboard	VCR
LCD projector	tape-recorder	computer
overhead projector	TV	other: _____

2 Which of the above do you have access to, but have chosen not to use? Why? Did you use those technologies in the past?

Task 2

An inappropriate use of the technology of video is to have large groups of pupils watch long stretches or entire movies together with very little preparation or follow-up. It is impossible to find a full-length video that will engage a large group for its entire duration and is aimed at a level appropriate for all viewers – some learners will invariably tune out. The result is often that pupils come to see video as a teacher's way of 'killing time,' and it ceases to be a useful and valid instructional tool.

1 What is your experience with using video in the classroom? Were videos used in any classes you attended as a pupil?

2 Although full-length films can certainly be shown effectively with the right group of learners and with appropriate preparation and follow-up, shorter videos may generally be more appropriate. Possibilities include:

- short (15 to 20 minutes) commercial videos prepared specifically for educational purposes;

- news clips, interviews, commercials, talk shows, music videos, documentaries, etc., of appropriate length (and recorded after appropriate permission has been obtained);

- short programmes (about 20 minutes, without commercials) that can be viewed in segments and thus form a constituent part of several lessons; and

- short programmes on topics of interest to pupils and relevant to their needs.

Have you used any of the above with your pupils? How successful were such recordings?

3 Video content should be analysed from the pupils' perspective. Will your pupils find it interesting and suitable? How does the content you select relate to pupils' own circumstances and goals? Do you ask pupils to discuss the topic prior to viewing, brainstorming ideas and predicting the content?

4 In addition to previewing activities, pupils need to be provided with a task to complete during viewing. This makes the activity more meaningful because it gives pupils a clear notion of why they are participating. Can you identify some of the tasks you have used, or list ideas for tasks that could be created?

Video: _____   Task: _____

Video: _____   Task: _____

Video: _____   Task: _____

⑤ If you have used such tasks, were they effective? How successfully did your pupils complete them while watching the video?

⑥ A videotape of your pupils made during a presentation activity can become a teaching tool in its own right. For example, teachers might record pupil presentations and ask learners to view the video to analyse their language use and presentation skills. Have you ever created such a learning tool in your classroom?

Computers

Computers in schools and their use in instruction provoke extreme reactions, ranging from enthusiasm to deep resentment. Teachers are generally either enthusiasts ('I can't wait for the new computers!'), mild supporters ('An excellent idea, but we'll need a lot of time to implement it'), quasi-supporters ('An excellent idea, but it won't work in my classroom'), passive resisters ('Not a bad idea, but very impractical'), or fierce opponents ('Another fancy way senior management have found to waste money'). Most of us, however, realise that computers are here to stay, and their role in education has increased significantly. ICT is now a part of the National Curriculum and controversy over its inclusion is beginning to diminish, and remaining opposition will probably turn into quiet acceptance.

This is appropriate, since the benefits of computers as an instructional tool are numerous. Nevertheless, as with any other piece of technology, caution is recommended with computers, too. We must ensure that when we use them we do so meaningfully. Despite all their advantages, the headaches of using this technology are many and varied, for both the teaching staff and the administration. They include the following areas of concern:

- the need for initial teacher training and education;
- the need for ongoing training with new equipment and software;
- substantial initial costs for hardware and software;
- ongoing costs associated with upgrades of hardware and software;
- the need for field-testing and evaluation of hardware, software, and instructional packages;
- problems of reliability; and
- ongoing reliance on technical support.

Some of the advantages and disadvantages related to computer use are explored in the following tasks.

Task 1

❶ Physical arrangements for making computers available to pupils and teachers vary considerably. Which of the options below best describes the situation in your teaching context?

☐ A shared computer lab of stand-alone terminals, available on a preset schedule.

☐ A shared computer lab of networked terminals, available on a preset schedule.

☐ A computer lab of networked or stand-alone terminals, available on a first-come, first-served basis.

☐ A single computer in my own classroom.

☐ Several computers in my own classroom.

❷ The physical set-up obviously has an effect on how computers can be used for individual, pair, group, or whole-class work, and for in-class, remedial, or homework activities. How do you maximise the opportunities for learning with the options that are available to you?

Task 2

Think about how you present and explain software to your pupils to ensure that they know how to use the program's features.

❶ What teaching techniques and strategies do you use when you present and explain a new software package or any unfamiliar features or functions it might contain? Indicate how often you use each of these possibilities.

☐ I photocopy and distribute pages from the manual ___% of the time.

☐ I write up and distribute a simple instruction sheet ___% of the time.

☐ Prior to class, I write instructions on the board or on a flipchart placed in a spot visible to everyone in class ___% of the time.

☐ I demonstrate the software and its functions to the class as a whole ___% of the time.

☐ I explain to all pupils while writing step-by-step instructions on the board, and then I circulate to provide support while the pupils work on their own ___% of the time.

☐ I demonstrate it sequentially to small groups of pupils who gather around ___% of the time.

☐ I provide both written instructions and a demonstration ___% of the time.

☐ I demonstrate it to every pupil individually ___% of the time.

☐ I demonstrate it to a group of high-ability pupils and ask them to be teacher assistants ___% of the time.

☐ I work at my networked terminal, and pupils can see what I'm doing on their own monitors ___% of the time.

☐ Other: _____

❷ What is the rationale behind your usual method of presentation and explanation?

❸ If the computers are not in your regular classroom, where and when do you present new software and explain new operations?

	Always	Often	Sometimes	Never
I provide all introductions and explanations before pupils go to the computer lab.	☐	☐	☐	☐
I provide a brief introduction in class, but the full explanation is offered while pupils are seated at computers in the lab.	☐	☐	☐	☐
I write instructions on the board or chart paper before pupils go to the lab, and they copy them down.	☐	☐	☐	☐
Everything related to computers takes place in the lab.	☐	☐	☐	☐

Task 3

We often have more pupils than computers in our classes, and this poses an additional challenge: who gets to use the computers when, and what do pupils do when they are not using them?

❶ What do you usually do in this situation?

☐ Two or more pupils sit together at the same machine.

☐ One pupil is seated at each computer, while others work on different tasks; after a predetermined length of time, pupils switch positions.

☐ Pupils are scheduled individually for computer time to perform the necessary tasks.

☐ Other: _____

❷ If you usually follow the second option above, how do you prepare?

☐ I have the activities ready prior to class.

☐ I make a decision about activities on the spot, depending on how many pupils are present in class.

☐ Other: _____

❸ You cannot be in two places at the same time. If some of your pupils are working on computers while others are in a different part of the room, engaged with other tasks, how do you handle the situation?

☐ I explain the computer task to the first group who will be working at the computers, then I leave them for a while to explain the other task to the second group (or vice versa); after that I assist whichever group seems to need more help.

☐ I explain the non-computer-related task, and then leave that group to work on their own because these tasks are usually easier to do than the computer work.

☐ Other: _____

❹ Do you clearly indicate in your lesson plan what each group will be doing and when?

Resources in the community

You and your pupils are members of communities that offer a variety of resources. By bringing those resources into the classroom – or bringing your classroom to them – you ensure your pupils' exposure to the most authentic learning material: people and places from the community.

Task 1

Place a tick beside the community resources you use in your search for materials for your teaching.

Community	Resources	How I use these resources
City/Town	☐ Municipal offices	_____
	☐ Cultural and recreational facilities	_____
	☐ Local newspapers	_____
	☐ Other	_____
Neighbourhood	☐ Community agencies	_____
	☐ Community publications	_____
	☐ Community services	_____
	☐ Community events	_____
	☐ Volunteers	_____
	☐ Guest speakers	_____
	☐ Other	_____
The school	☐ Administrative staff	_____
	☐ Colleagues	_____
	☐ Other classes and students	_____
	☐ Other	_____

Task 2

Do this task if you include field trips or guest speakers in your course.

❶ How do you decide what places to visit or who to invite to your class?

☐ I choose, according to my preferences.

☐ I evaluate the 'success rate' of previous trips or speakers.

☐ I pass around a list of suggested sites to visit or speakers to invite, and let pupils make selections.

☐ I choose places and people that can enhance the curriculum.

☐ I plan around pupils' needs and interests.

☐ Other: _____

❷ How do you prepare for field trips or guest speakers?

☐ I prepare pupils by teaching the main concepts and language.

☐ Pupils research the place or topic.

☐ I bring in promotional literature.

☐ I brainstorm what needs to be pretaught with the guest speaker or staff at the field trip site.

☐ I make clear to the speaker or site staff the proficiency level of the pupils.

☐ I talk to the guest speaker or site staff prior to the event and make suggestions intended to ensure that their presentation is as interactive and appropriate as possible.

☐ Other: _____

❸ If you teach older or more proficient pupils, do you make them part of the preparation? Do you ever ask them to contact a guest speaker and arrange a session?

❹ Complete the following chart.

	Always			Never	
	5	4	3	2	1
During the trip or guest speaker's presentation					
Pupils undertake a task I have planned and explained.	☐	☐	☐	☐	☐
I make myself available to the pupils and site staff or guest speaker.	☐	☐	☐	☐	☐
I monitor interaction and try to ensure that all pupils participate and are involved.	☐	☐	☐	☐	☐
I take notes during the presentation so that I can create follow-up activities later.	☐	☐	☐	☐	☐
Other: _____	☐	☐	☐	☐	☐
After the trip or presentation					
I ask the speaker or site staff for feedback on how my group reacted.	☐	☐	☐	☐	☐
I sum up experiences in a follow-up lesson.	☐	☐	☐	☐	☐
I obtain feedback from pupils.	☐	☐	☐	☐	☐
I make notes about any problems or things that should have been done differently, for future reference.	☐	☐	☐	☐	☐
Other: _____	☐	☐	☐	☐	☐

❺ Is there anything in your use of community resources that needs to be altered? If so, what?

Pupils as resources

Pupils bring to class a variety of experiences that teachers can and should draw on. Everybody has something to share – whether it is a talent in music or cooking, a fascinating cultural heritage, or professional knowledge – and we can all learn from that sharing. Further, giving pupils the opportunity to identify and give what they have to offer puts them in the position of experts and boosts their self-confidence.

Task 1

❶ How do you usually identify the expertise and experience your pupils may have? Can you recall expertise and experience among your pupils that you have tapped into recently or would like to explore?

Pupil: _____ Expertise/experience: _____

Pupil: _____ Expertise/experience: _____

Pupil: _____ Expertise/experience: _____

❷ Obviously, pupils are more motivated to participate in class if they can bring their own background knowledge, experiences, and circumstances into the discussions and activities. This applies to all learners, from beginners to advanced and from pre-school children to adults.

Analyse an activity you are planning to do with your pupils. What background knowledge might pupils have that relates to the activity? How can you activate that knowledge?

❸ How are you going to make use of this background knowledge? How will using it benefit the pupils?

Task 2

One way of having pupils share their expertise and experiences is to arrange for group or individual in-class presentations on appropriate topics and issues.

❶ Do you include group, pair, or individual presentations by pupils in your course? Why or why not?

❷ What kind of presentations do you include, and how often?

❸ How do you ensure that the audience is respectful and maintains interest?

❹ What language and communication skills necessary for presentations do you teach?

❺ What tasks do you give your pupils to complete while listening to the presentations?

❻ Do you expect your presenters to prepare handouts or to create tasks for the work an before, during, or after the presentation?

❼ Do your learners evaluate the presentations?   Yes ☐   No ☐

❽ If yes, do you generate the evaluation criteria with them?   Yes ☐   No ☐

❾ In what other ways do you invite pupils to share their expertise and experience with the class?

Task 3

Conduct an experiment in your class. Have your pupils prepare short group presentations on a topic of interest they know or want to research. Teach the necessary presentation skills, prepare the venue and the audience, and plan a listening task for class members to complete during each presentation. Observe your pupils' participation and motivation. Finally, survey your pupils on their feelings about the process. What are the results of the experiment?

Summary

In this chapter you have examined possible uses of resources and reflected on the resources you already use. You have considered the variety of resources you already use or might use in future. You have reflected on your use of technology and have considered how your use of resources might be improved. Copies of your responses to these tasks along with annotated lesson plans, student and colleague comments and audio- or video-tapes of lessons can be used in a professional development record to evidence your continuing professional development in the use of resources.

What is the difference between a good meal and a solid lesson? None, since both must include fresh, well-balanced ingredients, selected according to the consumers' preferences and needs. Successful lessons incorporate numerous ingredients essential to the learning process. The balance of those ingredients determines the quality of the lesson – which, in turn, determines the level of learning and the resulting pupil satisfaction. We must therefore make time for frequent contemplation of how the elements of our work in the classroom fit together. Decisions regarding preparation, delivery of instructions, classroom language, presentation techniques, and pacing are numerous, and each requires reflection. It is essential that we consider how all the possible options may affect our lessons – and pupils – before we actually step into the classroom.

There are no magic formulas for conducting effective lessons all the time. The reflection process might therefore appear quite elusive, particularly to novice teachers. Still, it is a highly beneficial undertaking, as it makes us better able to predict what might happen in the classroom and thereby to anticipate some potential problem areas.

This chapter is intended to encourage you not only to give attention to the quality of each of your lesson elements and the way they all work together, but also to evaluate your performance after lessons are completed and to establish goals for improvement.

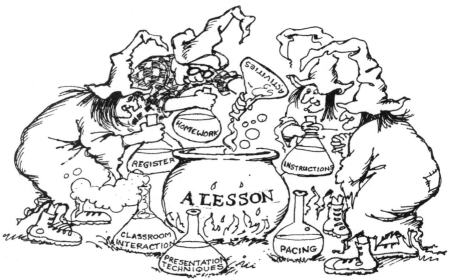

Presentation techniques and language

Two presentation techniques, inductive and deductive, were illustrated in Chapter 5 on lesson planning (see pp. 31). Additional aspects of presentation may include your choice of language and manner of speaking, the use of teaching aids, and your physical position in the classroom. (The latter is explored in greater detail in Chapter 3, where it is presented in the context of use of classroom space.)

Task 1

❶ Identify what you do in the classroom to ensure that pupils can hear and understand you and that their attention is held during your presentation.

	A lot				Not at all
	5	4	3	2	1
I vary my presentation techniques to include both inductive and deductive approaches.	☐	☐	☐	☐	☐
I use both aural and visual aids.	☐	☐	☐	☐	☐
I present concepts in a natural context.	☐	☐	☐	☐	☐
I monitor my voice to ensure clarity, audibility, and appropriate speed.	☐	☐	☐	☐	☐
I change position in the room – sometimes standing at the front, sometimes at the side, and sometimes circulating.	☐	☐	☐	☐	☐
I check with my pupils to make sure that they can all hear me well. I vary the tone and melody of my voice.	☐	☐	☐	☐	☐
I check frequently to ensure that my pupils understand the concepts I am presenting.	☐	☐	☐	☐	☐
I use an appropriate level of language.	☐	☐	☐	☐	☐
Other: _____	☐	☐	☐	☐	☐

❷ Which points above are your particular strengths? How are you going to address the weaknesses?

Task 2

Experts agree that, regardless of the level of learners, a teacher's language must be comprehensible and authentic, rather than artificial and unlike what one would hear outside the classroom. It has to be clearly articulated but should also expose pupils to new vocabulary, structures, expressions, and idioms. This is true for all classrooms from reception to sixth form.

❶ How do the points above relate to your use of language in the classroom?

❷ What do you think teachers should keep in mind about the use of language in the classroom?

❸ Monitor your language during presentations for the next few lessons. (If possible, do this by video- or audio-taping yourself and preparing transcripts of a few segments during which you spoke at reasonable length.) Are you actually doing what you thought you were doing? What are your strengths and weaknesses in language use?

Giving instructions

In order for an activity to be effective, pupils must understand the instructions. We have all had the experience of preparing solid activities that turn out to be less than successful because pupils did not understand what we wanted them to do. When we know that an activity is strong, we are often tempted to rush ahead to start it without adequate explanation, or we fail to plan how instructions will be delivered.

Giving solid instructions for a task does not involve special know-how, but it does require planning in advance of each activity. Self-evaluation guided by the checklist in Task 1 and the video-taping in Task 4 may be particularly effective in helping you to assess and improve your skills in this area.

Task 1

To ensure that all pupils understand the instructions, are on task, and are able to keep up with the class, which of these actions do you usually perform?

	Always			Never	
	5	4	3	2	1
I plan my strategies for explaining the task before I come to class.	☐	☐	☐	☐	☐
I wait to get attention from all my pupils before I start to deliver instructions.	☐	☐	☐	☐	☐
My instructions include information to ensure that pupils are absolutely clear about what they are supposed to do and why and are provided to all pupils simultaneously. I avoid repeating them to individuals while distributing handouts or books.	☐	☐	☐	☐	☐
My instructions are concise, clear, and ordered in a logical sequence and I support verbal instructions with visual aids and demonstration, if necessary.	☐	☐	☐	☐	☐
I am cautious about when I distribute books or other materials or ask pupils to open their texts, because I do not want to distract them from listening to me.	☐	☐	☐	☐	☐
I tell pupils how much time will be allotted to the activity.	☐	☐	☐	☐	☐
I make statements to trigger pupils' background knowledge related to the activity.	☐	☐	☐	☐	☐
I do a trial run through the activity with a group of pupils to provide an example.	☐	☐	☐	☐	☐
I don't assume that pupils have understood the instructions, but rather check directly that they have done so by asking *them* to explain what they are supposed to do.	☐	☐	☐	☐	☐

Task 2

Investing time in planning how instructions will be issued pays off in the long run. By constructing a clear picture of what needs to be explained and how, teachers avoid the scenario in which pupils spend the first five or ten minutes of the activity floundering in confusion and asking their classmates or the teacher for help. After all, when this does happen, the teacher has to come up with clearer instructions anyway. For pupils, unclear instructions mean time must be spent searching for strategies to decode the task, and obviously the opportunities for learning presented within the task itself may be obstructed.

❶ Select an upcoming activity and plan the instructions. What are you going to do and say? Go over the list in Task 1 and note the actions you plan to perform.

❷ Did rereading the list prompt you to think about any areas where there is room for improvement in your own practice?

Task 3

Pupils, like teachers, 'acquire classroom experience' – for them, this means learning how to learn and becoming familiar with different types of activities. 'Experienced' learners usually need less explanation and less time to carry out variations on familiar tasks. New activities, however, should be allotted more explanation and time since pupils are learning both *from* the task and the task *itself*.

Do you consider this when introducing activities? Think of the last time you used a type of activity you and your pupils had never used before. Did any problems occur? If so, was there anything you could have done to avoid them?

Task 4

❶ Video- or audio-tape one or two of your activities. While viewing or listening to the tape, focus on how you gave the instructions. Examine the list in Task 1 one more time, and note the actions you actually performed before your pupils plunged into the activity. (If taping is not possible, try to self-evaluate right after you conduct an activity.)

❷ Check the tape again and focus on your pupils. Are they doing what they were expected to do?

❸ Was anyone asking questions or looking for clarification? If so, what insight does that give you? Could anything have been done differently?

❹ What impact would a different approach have had?

❺ How would you rate your instructions about this activity for this particular group?

5   4   3   2   1

Very effective   Not effective

Types of activities

One good way of tackling the problem of boredom in the classroom is to use a wide variety of activities. This variety must be logical, however; a lesson needs to include a sequence of activities and techniques with a common objective.

Task 1

Review your lesson plans for the past two weeks and note the types of activities you used. Possibilities might include:

brainstorming	reading aloud	skimming
role-play	pair work	finding similarities/differences
hands-on manipulation	problem-solving	guessing game
discussion	questionnaire	opinion poll

lab activities and demonstrations	dialogue	matching
artwork	storytelling	cloze or fill in the blanks
songs	questions and answers	vocabulary practice
puzzles	sequencing	free writing
scanning	guided writing	completing a worksheet

❶ Was there enough variety in the activities you conducted? Yes ☐ No ☐

❷ Circle any activities on the list above that you are not familiar with. Where could you find out about them?

❸ Are there activities on the list that you rarely or never use? If so, which ones? Why?

❹ Is there any type of activity that you really feel uncomfortable doing? Why?

Task 2

Think about the activities you used in the past two weeks and consider the following questions.

❶ Did they focus on both form (controlled practice such as grammar exercises, arithmetic practice, questions and answers, true and false statements, matching, etc.) and meaning (discussion, unrehearsed role-plays, interviews, surveys, group problem-solving, etc.)?

Yes ☐ No ☐

2. What was the balance of teacher-directed versus pupil-centred work?

Teacher-directed ___% Pupil-centred ___%

3. Was this balance reasonable and effective?

Yes ☐ No ☐

4. Were the pupils involved in problem-solving?

Yes ☐ No ☐

5. Did you facilitate all pupils' participation during the activity and in the report-back phase?

Yes ☐ No ☐

Preparing pupils for activities

Not only do teachers need to prepare for activities – so do pupils. An activity cannot be effective if pupils are not provided with all the tools necessary to perform it.

Task 1

One way of finding out whether you have done sufficient preparatory work with your pupils is to evaluate an activity right after it is completed, and then brainstorm how you could profit from any errors in preparing your pupils when you next conduct a similar activity.

❶ How much time did you spend preparing your pupils for the activity?

5 to 10 minutes   10 to 20 minutes   20 to 30 minutes   More than 30 minutes

❷ What information, areas of the subject matter, skills, and strategies related to the activity did you teach before the activity?

❸ Was the preparation time enough?

Yes ☐   No ☐   Almost ☐

❹ Were most pupils able to cope with the activity without difficulty?

Yes ☐   No ☐   Almost ☐

❺ Did you monitor the process?

Yes ☐   No ☐

❻ Were pupils able to transfer and use knowledge gained before the activity in completing it?

Yes ☐   No ☐

❼ If your response to any of these questions was no, why?

❽ In the activity, were you teaching or testing?

❾ What, if anything, would you do differently next time?

Task 2

If learners are not prepared for the activity, the result is stress and frustration. Pupils respond to activities better if they know what they can expect and feel comfortable with the skills and material that have been taught before the activity.

❶ How do you help your pupils lower their level of stress and frustration?

❷ Have you ever noticed your pupils hesitating about starting work on an activity? Perhaps on occasion they leaf through their notebooks or books, look around in confusion, ask their classmates for help, or complain to each other. How would you describe the atmosphere? How do you think they felt?

❸ How did you react? Was your reaction appropriate?

❹ Do you remember experiencing stress in your own days as a pupil because you felt underprepared to accomplish an activity? What could your teachers have done to minimise this stress?

Pace

Classroom activities are not unlike visits from distant relatives. When they drag on too long, what began as the best of times can turn into a nightmare. And when they are too short, you feel that many stories you wanted to share remain untold.

To understand aspects of how to pace our teaching, we must consider the classroom experience. Novice teachers tend to cut an activity off when the time they had planned for it has elapsed; as a consequence, they can pass up opportunities to capitalise on pupils' interests. With experience, teachers learn to gauge their activities, continually checking how pupils are responding and developing a sense of exactly when to stop one activity and move along to the next. However, teachers can have a tendency to let an activity go on for too long, particularly when it's a good one they have taken a lot of time to prepare. It can be beneficial to stop an activity while pupils are still feeling 'I could have done that for longer.'

Task 1

❶ For your next lesson plan, use the chart below to note the time you plan to spend on each activity. As the lesson unfolds, mark the actual time spent. After the lesson, reflect on any digressions and the rationale for them, and re-evaluate the time originally allotted to each activity. (If possible, video-tape your lesson, and then view the tape to determine the time spent on the activities, the digressions, and possible ways to revise your pacing.) Note comments about pacing the activities on your lesson plan fc future reference.

Activity	Time allotted	Time spent	Digressions	Why?	Revised tim allotment

❷ Your pupils will certainly be willing to provide you with feedback on pacing. After one of your next lessons, explain to them that you want to ensure appropriate pacing, and ask them to complete a survey indicating whether each activity in the lesson was much too long, a little long, just right, a little short, or much too short. Analyse the survey results to determine whether the majority of the pupils felt there was a pacing problem in the lesson.

Task 2

A French teacher gave the pupils in her mixed-ability class a crossword puzzle to complete as a warm-up activity at the beginning of a lesson. The majority completed the task within the planned twenty minutes and started talking among themselves — which would have been good practice in conversation, except that they were speaking in English. Meanwhile, a few pupils were still trying to complete the puzzle. The activity dragged on for almost an hour, with the teacher going from one lower level pupil to the next to offer help. Her feeling was that these pupils, whose self-esteem was already low, would have felt badly had they not been able to finish the puzzle.

❶ What would you have done in this situation?

☐ I would have done what this teacher did.

☐ After the allotted time, I would have had pupils check their answers with other pupils, so that all would have obtained correct responses.

☐ I would have paired lower with higher level pupils.

☐ I would have given out two crossword puzzles of different levels of difficulty.

☐ I would have prepared an extra activity for higher level pupils.

☐ Other: _____

❷ What would the rationale for your action(s) be ?

Task 3

Even experienced teachers can misjudge the time required for a certain task. It often happens that some pupils finish well ahead of others, but we should never allow an activity to drag on because we can think of nothing else to do with the class. Experienced teachers usually plan additional tasks in case some or all pupils are able to complete an activity more quickly than planned, or they create two related activities, one easier and a second more challenging. They also develop a repertoire of review activities that need no introduction and may be used in conjunction with particular lessons – 'just in case'.

Analyse again (on video-tape, if possible) one of the activities analysed in Task 1.

❶ How many pupils finished the activity before the allotted time?

❷ Did they actually complete it, or did they simply lose interest?

❸ What were they doing after they finished?

❹ Did you notice any signs of boredom?

Yes ☐   No ☐   I don't know ☐

❺ What did you come up with to keep the learners who finished early busy and interested?

❻ If you have a mixed-ability class, what impact does it have on pacing?

Task 4

❶ Think back to your days as a pupil. When you did not participate in a lesson, what were the reasons?

☐ The lesson was too easy.

☐ I found the lesson too difficult or overwhelming.

☐ The lesson was not interesting.

☐ The lesson was not relevant to my needs.

☐ I simply did not want to participate.

☐ I did not like the teacher.

☐ Other: _____

❷ What did you do?

❸ How will you address the same problem in your class?

Activity evaluation

Unfortunately, there is no 'undo button' on the classroom keyboard – all we can do is try 'restart' the next time around. The effects of an activity that did not bring the desired results cannot be reversed, but we can ensure that the same thing does not happen again. Since we all seem to learn best from our own mistakes, one way to do this is to analyse an activity that did not work well with your pupils. Tasks 1 and 2 below are related in general to such an activity; subsequent tasks will help you consider each of the activity's stages.

Task 1

Reflect on why an unsuccessful activity was not productive and consider how it could be altered. (If you cannot remember any such activity, keep this task in mind to use when you realize that something has 'bombed'). Alternately, if you have already video- or audio-taped lessons for completion of earlier tasks, select the tape that contains the least successful activity and evaluate it by answering the questions below.

❶ What was the activity's objective?

❷ Did the whole lesson ultimately direct pupils toward this objective?

❸ Describe what you were doing during the activity.

❹ How would you define your role? Do you think anything related to your role needed to be altered?

Task 2

Imagine that you have found an excellent piece of text that contains a great deal of information relevant to the unit you are teaching. Unfortunately, the text is above your pupils' comprehension level and contains considerable unfamiliar vocabulary. If you decide to use the article, you will need to make some decisions *prior* to conducting the activity:

- What will be done as an introduction?

- How are you going to deal with the reading aspect? Will you read the text aloud? Will pupils read silently? Will pupils take turns reading one or two sentences aloud? Will that be done with the whole class or in groups? Will pupils be allowed to read silently prior to reading aloud?

- How are you going to deal with vocabulary? Will you ignore teaching it directly and instead concentrate on strategies of guessing and predicting? How will you explain to your pupils that they do not need to understand every word to get the gist of the text?

- In the event you want to present the vocabulary, how will that be done? Will pupils have access to dictionaries? If not, will you answer individual vocabulary questions while pupils read? Or will you perhaps ask pupils to make a list of unfamiliar words to be discussed after everyone has read the text?

- When discussing the vocabulary, will you present all of it on the board? Or will you present only selected vocabulary? Or will pupils work on it in pairs or groups?

- Finally, what is the task that pupils will do in relation to this text?

When planning an activity, most teachers think in terms of the first and last questions, and tend to neglect the ones in between.

❶ Reflect on decisions you made while planning the unsuccessful activity analysed in the preceding task. How detailed were your decisions at the lesson-planning stage?

❷ What can be the consequence of not making decisions prior to the lesson?

❸ Select a text to work on with your class. Now, neglect all the planning stages except the last one, and identify only the task itself. Conduct the activity, and observe your process of decision-making as you move along (or later, on a video-tape). What decisions are you forced to make? What impact do they have on the class? What impact would different decisions have had on your class?

Task 3

Now do a detailed, stage-by-stage evaluation of the activity. Again, if you have the activity on tape, your analysis can be considerably more objective.

❶ What introductory activity did you do to focus the pupils' attention?

❷ What strategies were your pupils expected to use to complete the activity? How did the warm-up prepare pupils to use the strategies successfully?

❸ In setting the task, were instructions concise, clear, and specific enough? How do you know?

❹ Were all your pupils absolutely clear about what they were supposed to do? How did you check this before starting the activity?

❺ Was the activity engaging for your pupils? Did all of them participate?

❻ If interaction was part of the task, did this go well?

❼ In your follow-up, did you elicit pupils' reactions to the activity? Did you check if they enjoyed it? What part of it did they find most useful?

❽ Was the activity set at the right level – challenging enough, but not too difficult for the majority of pupils? If not, how could it be modified to better suit your pupils?

❾ Was it well paced? What do you think is the most effective length of time for this activity?

Task 4

Now consider where your pupils' problems with the activity originated, with a view to improving your facilitation.

❶ Which cues helped your pupils perform the activity?

❷ Where did the pupils have trouble?

❸ What help did they ask for?

❹ If the activity involved a text, how did you deal with new concepts, vocabulary, or comprehension problems?

❺ What follow-up activities did you do?

Task 5

Finally, think of ways in which the activity could have been improved.

1 Based on your responses in the preceding tasks, can you identify the reason(s) why the activity was unsuccessful?

2 If so, how could you revise the activity, knowing what you do now?

3 In which areas do your pupils need more practice before you undertake such an activity again?

4 Did your pupils suggest variations to the activity? Did you ask them to?

Summary

In this chapter you have reflected on the various elements of your lessons. You have considered your presentations style, how you deliver instructions, evaluated activities that you use and examined the pace of your lessons. Copies of your responses to these tasks along with annotated lesson plans, student and colleague comments and audio- or video-tapes of lessons and examples of activities you have created or evaluated can be used in your professional development record to provide evidence of your continuing professional development in this area.

One of our jobs as teachers is to help pupils identify and achieve their own educational goals, and an element necessary for future success is the ability to communicate and cooperate well with others. Meaningful interaction should therefore be one of the cornerstones on which classroom work is built.

At various times during a lesson, pupils may be involved in individual, pair, or group work, or they may do whole-class activities or listen while the teacher or another pupil makes a presentation. Each of these patterns of interaction is valuable, and pupils benefit from variety and balance among them. This chapter discusses how to assess whether that balance is being achieved and whether the interactive situations in your classroom are successful.

Patterns of interaction

Task 1

Reflect on the patterns of interaction in your last few lessons. Use the circle below to create a pie chart indicating the percentage of time, on average, your pupils spent in individual, pair, group, and whole-class activities.

Now sum up your observations.

❶ Do you vary patterns of interaction?

　　Yes ☐　　No ☐　　Not always ☐

❷ How do you encourage pair, group, and whole-class interaction?

❸ How do you encourage team work?

Task 2

Teachers are human, and some (ourselves included) may tend to talk too much. After all, we always have something *very* important to say! A possible rule of thumb for establishing a balance between teacher and pupil talk is 'If a pupil can say what you want to say, try not to say it yourself, but make sure you repeat or clarify what the pupil says so that everyone in class understands.'

① Could this rule be applied in your class? To what extent?

② Try to determine if, in general, you are a 'talker.'

☐ People say I talk a lot, but I disagree.

☐ People say I talk a lot, and I agree.

☐ No one has ever commented on the amount of talking I do, so I assume my talk time is well balanced.

☐ People say I'm too quiet.

③ How much do you think you talk in class?

More than necessary ☐   Only as much as necessary ☐   Less than necessary ☐

④ Is there a clash between your answers to questions 2 and 3? If so, why?

⑤ Record a representative segment from a lesson. Play back the recording and use a stopwatch to time the teacher and pupil talk. Do the data prove or disprove your responses to the preceding questions?

⑥ If you feel you are perhaps too talkative in class, try to minimise your talk time for several days. What impact does this have on class interaction?

⑦ Survey your pupils. How do they feel about teacher and learner talk? Do they feel there is a balance in your class? Do they think that pupil talk is valuable and conducive to learning?

Group work

It is only in the past thirty or forty years that educators have discovered and come to appreciate the potential of group work. Regardless of the benefits, however, there are still many traditional 'teacher-fronted' classrooms, and many pupils (especially adults and children from various cultural backgrounds) may be unfamiliar with how to work in a group.

To introduce your pupils to group work, you might begin by explaining some of its benefits. In *Getting Pupils to Talk*, Aleksandra Golebiowska lists several:

- it generates more pupil talking-time than any other technique;
- it frees the teacher to teach more effectively;
- it is learner-centred and thus actively involves all learners;
- it makes learners responsible for their own learning;
- it is beneficial to the development of group dynamics.

To these could be added:

- it allows more natural pupil–pupil interaction rather than just teacher–pupil interaction;
- it frees the pupils from dependence on the teacher.

Task 1

❶ How do you form groups? Rank order the options below according to how often you use them.

☐ Pupils choose whom they would like to work with.

☐ Groups are determined by the seating arrangement and never changed.

☐ I group pupils according to a single criterion (e.g., age, ability level, etc.).

☐ I group pupils according to different criteria at different times.

☐ We do a group-forming activity or game.

☐ Other:

❷ What criteria do you apply for group formation? From the list below, choose the five options you use most frequently, and write the percentage of time you use each of them.

☐ Random grouping ＿＿＿ %

☐ Need for groups of a certain size ＿＿＿ %

☐ Seating arrangements ＿＿＿ %

☐ Ability ＿＿＿ %

☐ Pupils' own selections ＿＿＿ %

☐ Friendship ＿＿＿ %

☐ Common interests ＿＿＿ %

☐ Age ＿＿＿ %

☐ Ethnic origin ＿＿＿ %

☐ First language ＿＿＿ %

☐ Deliberately mixed ＿＿＿ %

☐ Other: ＿＿＿＿＿＿＿＿＿＿＿＿＿＿＿＿＿＿＿＿＿

❸ What single criterion do you use most frequently to group your pupils? Why?

❹ Experiment in a few upcoming lessons by using grouping criteria that you do not usually use. Do they work well? Is there a need for change in the criteria you use?

Task 2

Random grouping incorporates a positive element of surprise: pupils never know who they will be working with, and are usually quite accepting of their groups. The drawback, however, is that the teacher can only guess how the particular groupings will work.

❶ Indicate which of the following procedures for establishing random groups you have used.

☐ Pupils 'number off' or are each given a colour, letter, etc., and form groups according to numbers, colours, or letters they share.

☐ Pupils are asked to get together with others wearing something of the same colour.

☐ Groups are determined by alphabetical order of first or last names: the first four pupils form one group, the second four the second group, etc.

☐ Pupils are asked to find others with whom they have never or rarely worked, who live close to them, who like the same type of food, etc.

☐ Each pupil is given a piece of a picture (related to the topic being taught) and has to get together with pupils who have the other pieces.

☐ Other: _____

❷ Is there a technique that you have not used but would like to try?

Task 3

This task is related to group size.

❶ What is your preferred number of pupils in a group?

3   4   5   6   more than 6

❷ Why?

❸ Try to change that number during your next teaching day. Monitor what difference this makes. How did it affect the group work in regard to pupil talk and task completion?

Task 4

Grouping by ability has different benefits and drawbacks. Equal-ability groups ensure that weaker learners are not inhibited by more able ones, who themselves are not held back by weaker peers. Mixed-ability groups allow pupils to learn from one another and give pupils at higher proficiency levels a chance to enjoy being 'experts'.

If you use ability grouping, what are its strengths and weaknesses for your learners? If you do not, might your pupils benefit from it?

Task 5

❶ Use the chart below to evaluate group dynamics and the quality of participation of individual pupils in one of your next lessons. Observe group interaction carefully or, if possible, video or audiotape the group activity. We suggest that you focus on just *one* group so that you can monitor interaction during the whole activity. After the lesson, ask the pupils in that particular group to complete the chart as well. If you taped the activity, play it back. If you had to complete the chart again, would you pick the same numbers?

	Yes				No
	5	4	3	2	1
All group members contributed equally.	☐	☐	☐	☐	☐
Pupils were truly involved and motivated.	☐	☐	☐	☐	☐
Pupils found the activity interesting.	☐	☐	☐	☐	☐
The atmosphere in the group was positive and conducive to learning.	☐	☐	☐	☐	☐
Pupils were communicating well and clearly.	☐	☐	☐	☐	☐
Pupils were using newly acquired information or skills.	☐	☐	☐	☐	☐

❷ Use the points in the chart to develop a survey for your pupils to solicit their opinions and attitudes about group work. What are their responses?

Reflect on the things you do in order to make efficient use of the time devoted to group work.

❶ Do you define the activity for the whole class and avoid explaining it to each group individually?

Yes ☐   No ☐   Not always ☐

❷ Do you circulate while your pupils are performing the activity?

Yes ☐   No ☐   Not always ☐

❸ Circle the word that best describes your role when you circulate.

consultant   helper   observer   controller   other: _____

❹ Check with your pupils. Do they see you in the same role as you see yourself? Would they like you to assume a different role?

❺ Do you initiate the group interaction, or do the pupils?

❻ In what cases do you involve yourself in the group's interaction?

❼ Do you take note of errors pupils make while working on the activity?

Yes ☐   No ☐   Not always ☐

❽ If you do, do you follow up with activities to assist pupils in correcting those mistakes?

Yes ☐   No ☐   Not always ☐

Dealing with learner differences

Most of us daydream on occasion of an ideal class of uniform pupils with no individual differences. The fact that, in reality, every group consists of learners of different abilities, preferences, needs and backgrounds puts considerable demands on us. At the same time, though, it does make our job interesting and challenging. After all, if our pupils were all the same, we could be replaced by computers, couldn't we?

Ensuring effective interaction in a group of mixed-ability pupils is a juggling act – we cannot make everyone happy at the same time, and someone will always have to compromise. There are, however, ways of attempting the impossible.

There are various ways to ensure that most (if not all) pupils in your class are busy and challenged and that everyone receives individual attention.

❶ Look at the list below and indicate the techniques or approaches you have found most beneficial in ensuring that all pupils receive some individual attention. Think about which ones you have used recently.

Technique	Very beneficial			Not beneficial	
	5	4	3	2	1
Assigning frequent partner or group work	☐	☐	☐	☐	☐
Circulating during partner or group work	☐	☐	☐	☐	☐
Encouraging helpful, knowledgeable pupils to work with less proficient ones on occasion	☐	☐	☐	☐	☐
Journal writing	☐	☐	☐	☐	☐
Providing individualised tasks	☐	☐	☐	☐	☐
Designing activities at different levels of complexity that allow pupils to work at their own level and pace	☐	☐	☐	☐	☐
Providing follow-up activities for higher level pupils (lower ability pupils may do them as homework)	☐	☐	☐	☐	☐
Having a stock of extra activities on hand	☐	☐	☐	☐	☐
Using learning centres so that pupils can choose activities	☐	☐	☐	☐	☐
Other: _____	☐	☐	☐	☐	☐

❷ Do you think that each of your pupils feels he or she is getting enough individual attention to ensure that his or her needs are met?

Yes ☐   No ☐

❸ If you answered 'No,' what will you do to better accommodate these pupils?

Team building, racial tensions, and conflict resolution

Classrooms today are increasingly diverse places. Among our goals, therefore, should be promoting sensitivity to and understanding of different cultures and values.

Task 1

Understanding of different backgrounds and support for a diversity of pupils begins with raising awareness of distinctive features of cultures represented in your classroom. Some features relate to deeply held value and belief systems, while others are manifested in behaviour, clothing, and habits.

❶ What differences can you identify among your pupils pertaining to the following?

Eye contact: _____

Conversational distance: _____

Body language: _____

Use of time/punctuality: _____

Physical contact: _____

Attire: _____

Loudness of speaking: _____

Other: _____

❷ Imagine that you are one of your pupils who is a member of a visible minority. List several barriers or difficulties that this pupil may experience in your or any other class because of his or her background.

❸ What have you done or could you do to assist this pupil?

Task 2

Experienced teachers are often able to maximise opportunities for developing positive attitudes toward other cultures, thereby minimising the possibility of classroom conflict arising from intolerance or ignorance of cultural differences. Think about what you do in your classroom to build rapport among pupils, eliminate racial tensions and discrimination, and encourage mutual respect.

❶ Have you been able to create a harmonious classroom environment?

❷ What could you do to reduce negative attitudes and interactions?

❸ Do you use activities that encourage pupils to interact and mingle with peers of backgrounds different from their own?

❹ Through the material you use, do you sometimes offer your pupils a vision of the world from a perspective different from their own?

❺ How do you encourage pupils to further one another's cultural education in the classroom?

Task 3

Consider how you may have handled conflict in the past.

❶ Have there been any incidents of conflict, racial tension, or discrimination in your classroom recently? If so, how many? What type of incidents?

❷ Consider one incident in particular. How did you react?

❸ In how many cases were you satisfied with how you handled the incidents? In how many cases were the involved pupils satisfied with the results or solution? What conclusions can you draw that might help you deal with such situations in future?

❹ To familiarise yourself with different cultures and prepare yourself to handle possible negative incidents, which of the following have you done?

☐ Attended workshops.

☐ Taken a course.

☐ Read appropriate literature.

☐ Consulted with colleagues.

☐ Sought advice from consultants or specialists in the field, social workers, etc.

☐ Approached appropriate groups in the community.

☐ Other: _____

Dealing with discipline problems

Pupils and teachers alike live in today's hectic world of rapid change, of too much work, far-flung and broken families, alienation from community, and widespread violence. No wonder discipline is becoming a burning issue and one of the main causes of frustration for teachers, especially those working in primary and secondary school environments in large cities.

If you teach in such a setting or are faced with issues related to discipline in your classes, you know that there is no magical way to deal with the inevitable problems. Instead, you must possess a repertoire of tools and techniques for different occasions.

Task 1

❶ The advice in the following list comes from both experienced teachers and secondary school pupils. Think about your own strengths and weaknesses in relation to disciplining, and place an *S* (strength) or *W* (weakness) beside each item to indicate how well it relates to you.

☐ Be consistent in everything you do.

☐ Practise what you preach.

☐ Don't just set the rules – stand by them.

☐ Apply the same rules to everyone in class – no favouritism.

☐ Decide what you want to accomplish, reveal these goals to the pupils, and act with conviction.

☐ Make your expectations clear to everyone (and, again, be consistent).

☐ Plan enough activities to keep pupils busy, and have extras ready for those who finish early.

☐ Try to make activities interesting and relevant to pupils' needs.

☐ Try to demonstrate understanding for your pupils, but at the same time be firm (especially at the beginning of a course).

☐ No matter what, do not lose your calm.

☐ Use a firm voice, but do not yell or scream.

☐ Do not confront an unruly pupil in front of the class, but rather talk to him or her in private.

☐ Use humour to dissipate tension and frustration.

☐ Involve the pupil, parents, and senior management in conflict resolution, if you can.

☐ If you're having a bad day, do not bring it to the classroom.

☐ Don't take things personally.

❷ If you noted any weaknesses, which would you like to correct first? Create an action plan to work on this area.

Task 2

Video-tape a few random lessons. When you play back the tape, focus on pupil behaviour and your reactions. Were there instances of misbehaviour? If so, analyse the segments and answer the following questions.

❶ What happened? What did the pupil(s) do? What did you do?

❷ Can you determine the reason for the misbehaviour?

❸ How could this behaviour be prevented in future?

❹ Are you pleased with your handling of the situation?   Yes ☐   No ☐   To some extent ☐

❺ If the situation were repeated, would your reaction be different?

Task 3

The chart below contains a list of some cues related to pupil behaviour. Have you observed these (or others) in your classroom? How do you interpret them? Complete columns 2 and 3 to help you consider possible ways to react to such behaviour in future.

Pupil cues	Your interpretation	Possible reactions
Pupils talk while I'm talking.		
Pupils look confused.		
Pupils are disruptive.		
Pupils ask others for help.		
Pupils write while I'm talking.		
Pupils flip through their notes.		
Pupils nod their heads.		
Pupils look around.		
Pupils laugh while I'm talking.		
Pupils yawn.		
Pupils leave their desks.		
Pupils don't do what is expected of them.		
Pupils are lethargic.		

Task 4

For many of us, pupil misbehaviour is our main frustration. For some, it affects and upsets us so deeply that we find ourselves on a one-way street: we can neither determine the causes nor find effective solutions. That is when peer consultation and observation can help, or at least relieve some of the tension.

If you are in such a situation, enlist a colleague in an experiment: each of you video-tape one or two of your lessons, and then exchange tapes. While watching them, you can both refer to the questions in Task 2. As a follow-up, offer each other a constructive analysis and advice pertaining to reactions and strategies that could be used more, and those that could be used less.

Classroom confidence and trust

Classroom confidence and trust is the invisible web that bonds pupils with one another and the teacher, that supports everyone with the knowledge that teaching will match learning, that emotional support is always available, and that things can and will get done effectively. Classroom confidence is a response to pupils' concerns of 'Can we do it? Can we get results? Is help going to be there when we need it?' and teachers' questions that ask, 'Can we manage this? Do the pupils (and their parents) respect and support us? Are they committed enough?' We know confidence and trust are there when our pupils say, 'We really missed you!' after a supply teacher has taught for a day. When they are lacking, the result is dissatisfaction on the part of teacher and pupils and a frustrating feeling that the lesson is not enjoyable or beneficial enough.

Even though many teachers manage to build classroom confidence and trust with every group of pupils, they cannot achieve it to the same extent each time. Seasoned practitioners can all recall groups of pupils that just 'clicked' with them right at the beginning of school year, and with whom bonds were strengthened in each new lesson. They also most probably remember at least one group for which it took a painstaking length of time to establish a solid relationship.

An experienced observer can sense the level of classroom confidence within ten minutes of entering a teaching setting; it can be felt in the air and seen on the teacher's and pupils' faces. Needless to say, pupils have a sixth sense for it, too.

Task 1

Classroom confidence involves several ingredients that help intensify class ties:

- building your own confidence – looking and acting confident, being aware of who you are and what you can do (the confidence you project is contagions);

- building your pupils' confidence – awareness of who your pupils are and their abilities, providing opportunities for pupils to feel confident about their work, reinforcing the reason you are all in the classroom; and

- building confidence that class work can and will get done – possession of the necessary knowledge of the subject matter and teaching methodologies, determination to achieve your goals.

1 Try to rate yourself on each of the 'building' elements listed above.

	Excellent			Poor	
	5	4	3	2	1
Building my own confidence	☐	☐	☐	☐	☐
Building pupils' confidence	☐	☐	☐	☐	☐
Building confidence about class work	☐	☐	☐	☐	☐

2 Which of the three building skills is your strongest?

3 To what extent do you feel that classroom confidence is present in your class?

4 If you feel that the level of confidence and trust could be improved, think about the three building elements and come up with an action plan for accomplishing this.

Summary

In this chapter you have thought about the communication in your classroom. You have considered the interactions between yourself and your pupils and those between your pupils. Copies of your responses to these tasks along with annotated lesson plans, student and colleague comments and audio- or video-tapes of lessons and the observation comments of peers and management can be used in your professional development record as evidence of your continuing professional development in this area.

A great deal of interaction in the classroom is initiated through questions and,answers. The quality of our questions and how we ask them profoundly affects the quality of pupil responses and ensuing discussion. Similarly, the way we respond to our pupils' questions – and the way they respond to ours – has a tremendous impact on the classroom atmosphere and pupil learning.

Teacher questions

Few aspects of teaching have been the focus of as much attention and research as teacher questions. Indeed, knowing how and when to ask appropriate questions is considered among our most important skills. With the introduction of video- and audio-taping in the classroom, practically every teacher can (and should) examine with considerable objectivity this aspect of his or her teaching. The results of self-evaluation in this area can be dramatic, since even minor changes in questioning techniques can have very positive effects.

Task 1

Analyse the types of questions you ask.

❶ Do you try to ask questions that require more than a one- or two-word response?

Yes, deliberately ☐   No, not consciously ☐

❷ How often do you ask thought-provoking questions in which pupils are challenged to think about and express their opinions?

Often ☐   Sometimes ☐   Rarely ☐   Never ☐

❸ How often do you ask questions aimed at determining if pupils understand your lesson or a text?

Often ☐   Sometimes ☐   Rarely ☐   Never ☐

❹ Do you know what the answers will be before you ask the question?

Always ☐   Often ☐   Sometimes ☐   Rarely ☐   Never ☐

❺ Do you ask questions that anticipate responses from more than one pupil (e.g., 'Who's seen the film version of this play? What did you all think of it?') and then allow time for answers and discussion?

Always ☐   Often ☐   Sometimes ☐   Rarely ☐   Never ☐

❻ Do you use pupils' responses to diagnose the areas within the subject matter that may require more work?

Always ☐   Often ☐   Sometimes ☐   Rarely ☐   Never ☐

Task 2

Try to examine different types of questions you use and their benefits for different pupils in various lessons. While working on your next lesson plan, write down ten questions you plan to ask. After the lesson, refer to the list to determine whether you actually asked the questions and, if so, consider the effect your questioning had. (If possible, video- or audio-tape the lesson so that your answers will be more objective and accurate.)

❶ List your questions.

_____ _____

_____ _____

_____ _____

_____ _____

_____ _____

❷ What types of questions are they? Enter the appropriate number for each category.

Yes-or-no questions: _____

Short-answer questions: _____

Long-answer questions: _____

❸ How much time did your pupils need to respond to your questions?

❹ Were your questions clearly worded?

Yes ☐   No ☐

❺ Were your questions worded to encourage pupil response?

Yes ☐   No ☐

❻ Were your questions phrased in the sort of language you would use outside of the classroom? Why or why not?

❼ Analyse a question your pupils had trouble with. What factors made that question challenging?

❽ Do you think your questioning skills could be improved? If so, how will you go about improving them?

Task 3

Research has identified two types of questions used by teachers in the classroom:

1. Questions whose answers are known to the teacher.

2. Questions whose answers are unknown to all parties.

Clearly, when we ask the second type of question in the classroom we stand a greater chance of prompting real-life interaction among pupils. Such questions also generally result in more complex, lengthy answers. The first type of question, however, also has an important role to play. One challenge of teaching children or teenagers lies in holding their attention when we need to explain new content. These questions can be used during explanation as a follow-up to the key points being presented. This makes pupils focus on what is being explained in anticipation of being questioned, which may help establish a lively rhythm in this phase of the lesson.

❶ Of the questions you listed in Task 2, how many are Type 1 and how many are Type 2?

1 _____ 2 _____

❷ For what purposes do you use these types of questions in your lessons?

Type 1. _____

Type 2. _____

Task 4

Research has indicated that we use significantly more imperatives and statements – and fewer questions – in the classroom than we do in our real-life interactions (Nunan & Lamb, 1996). Also, we use more questions that encourage only a short response.

❶ Video- or audio-tape a lesson. Review the tape, and select a segment during which you interact with your pupils. Count the number of imperatives, statements, and yes-no or short-answer questions you use.

Imperatives _____

Statements _____

Yes-no/short-answer questions_____

❷ Evaluate the quality of interaction in this segment. Do you think there is anything that needs to be changed? Would the interaction have been significantly improved if you had asked different questions?

❸ In an upcoming lesson, try to use more of Type 2 questions. What do you notice?

Common errors

It would be impossible to write down all the questions you plan to ask in a lesson and to analyse the implications of each one. The type of questions and the way they are asked often depends on how the lesson unfolds – on the way pupils respond and the unplanned things that happen. We also need to take into consideration that teaching is an 'on-line' process, and during a lesson we are usually thinking more about content than about questions. Thus, errors in questioning are inevitable. Consider the following scenarios:

- a primary school teacher followed up each of her questions with a series of three or four more questions intended to clarify and help pupils understand the initial question. She was puzzled by the fact that she often did not get the responses she expected;
- an ESL teacher asked his pupils, 'What do you think about the police in this area?' Without pausing, he continued, 'How did you like the policeman who was a guest speaker here? Was he nice? Yes? No?' The pupils looked on in confusion;
- on Monday morning, a secondary school teacher entered his class and, without focusing on anyone in particular, said, 'How was your weekend? Was it busy? Nice? Or busy and nice, 'cause sometimes being busy can be nice?' He was met by silence.

If you had been a pupil in one of these classes, how would you have reacted? In the first instance, the teacher failed to realise that pupils were responding to the question they held in memory – that is, the last one. And since this was much more focused and specific than the initial 'main' question, the pupils' responses were not what the teacher had hoped. In the second case, the teacher gave his pupils no time to process the questions he asked, which were a jumble of long-, short-, and one-word answers. And in the third, the teacher seemed to be rambling, perhaps out of nervousness at the possibility of conversational silence.

Task 1

The teachers described above would have benefited from taping and analysing question–answer portions of their interaction with pupils. If you have access to recording equipment, make a tape and transcribe a segment of questions and answers. If this is not possible, try to complete this task after careful reflection on how questioning works with your pupils.

❶ In your last few lessons, how often did you make the following errors in questioning?

	Often	Sometimes	Never
I did not give pupils enough time to process questions, but started assisting them right away.			
I looked at one pupil when I asked a question, then confused him or her by calling on someone else to answer.			
I asked questions that were too easy, and pupils put no effort into their responses.			
I asked questions that pupils did not understand, so I had to reword them.			
I asked and answered my own rhetorical questions.			
My questions were inappropriate (e.g., they asked for too much personal disclosure).			
I asked some pupils noticeably more questions than others.			
I posed sequential questions, giving pupils inadequate time to process each of them and no reason to respond.			

❷ From a pupil's perspective, which of the above do you think is the worst-case scenario? Why?

❸ How do you think pupils feel about rhetorical questions? How do you think you would react to them if you were a pupil?

❹ In your analysis of your questioning, what strengths have been revealed?

I ALWAYS MAKE SURE MY STUDENTS ARE PROVIDED WITH ENOUGH TIME TO THINK ABOUT MY QUESTIONS.

Pupil participation and responses

We have all conducted or observed classes where pupils spend most of their time in silence, speaking only when called on, where a few outspoken pupils dominate, or where everyone speaks at once. Teachers' skills in questioning can improve these sorts of classroom atmospheres and have a profound effect on the quality of pupil responses.

Task 1

Try to monitor which pupils are responding to your questions. In your next lesson, use an existing class list and cross off the names of any pupils who are absent. As you conduct the lesson, place a tick next to the names of pupils who respond to your questions or prompts. (You can use the same technique while playing back a tape of a previously recorded lesson.)

1. Did you call on any pupils more often than others?

    Yes ☐   No ☐

2. Did all pupils get equal amounts of your attention?

    Yes ☐   No ☐

3. Did you neglect any of your pupils?

    Yes ☐   No ☐

4. If yes, whom? Why?

5. How did you demonstrate interest in your pupils' responses?

6. Did any pupils not participate at all? If so, why do you think this was the case?

7. Have any patterns surfaced? Are you satisfied with them? If not, what could you change?

Task 2

Try to identify the factors that influence decisions about who will respond to your questions.

❶ What approach do you take?

	Always	Sometimes	Rarely	Never
I try to pick up my pupils' signals and ask only those who want to respond.	☐	☐	☐	☐
I ask pupils to raise their hands.	☐	☐	☐	☐
I call on pupils at random.	☐	☐	☐	☐
I call names according to a previously prepared plan.	☐	☐	☐	☐
Learners respond following their seating pattern.	☐	☐	☐	☐
Other: _____	☐	☐	☐	☐

❷ What is the rationale behind your usual approach?

❸ As a follow-up, create a survey with the above-listed options for your pupils, to determine their preferences.

Task 3

In every class, there are pupils who are noisier and more talkative than others. They tend to 'grab the microphone' and monopolise interaction. Novices beware! Finding effective ways of cutting down these pupils' talk time can be difficult, but it is essential to do so in order to ensure that all pupils get a chance to take part.

❶ One possibility is to re-word what a dominating pupil says, let him or her know that you appreciate the input, and then state directly that you would like to find out what other pupils think about the issue. Can you think of other approaches?

❷ Have you encountered similar situations? What approach did you take? Was it effective?

Task 4

Besides talkative pupils, every class includes learners with low self-esteem. Teachers must make special, but sensitive, efforts to draw these pupils into discussion.

❶ Which of the following do you do to make insecure pupils feel comfortable while participating in class?

☐ I ask questions that require different levels of proficiency to ensure that shy or lower level pupils can experience success.

☐ I always offer praise and encouragement, even if performance is lacking.

☐ I talk to those pupils individually before or after class to offer encouragement.

☐ I monitor grouping patterns to ensure that shy pupils are not 'dwarfed' by outgoing and noisy ones.

Other: _____

❷ Are you content with the way you are dealing with shy pupils?

Yes ☐   To some extent ☐   There's room for improvement ☐

Wait time and listening

In order to be effective communicators, we need to have good listening skills. Being a good listener in the classroom implies two things: giving pupils enough 'wait time' to process your questions, and displaying willingness to hear what they have to say. Obviously, pupils cannot express themselves if we are not patient and attentive ourselves.

Task 1

Reviewing a video- or audio-tape of a few of your lessons may help you answer the following questions. If this is not an option, try to recall how you handled aspects of waiting and listening in your last few lessons.

❶ How much time do you usually wait for a response to a yes/no question before you help the pupil or ask someone else?

1 second ☐   2 seconds ☐   3 or more seconds ☐

❷ How much time do you usually wait for the response to an open-ended question before you help the pupil or ask someone else?

1 second ☐   2 seconds ☐   3 or more seconds ☐

❸ Once a pupil has answered, how much time do you usually wait before posing another question?

1 second ☐   2 seconds ☐   3 or more seconds ☐

❹ If your response to any of the three preceding questions was '1 second,' try to prolong the wait time during one of your next lessons. Did it have an effect? If so, describe it.

Pupil questions

If real learning is to take place, pupils must be able to ask for explanations, clarification, or repetition. This communication skill is even more crucial outside the classroom. We should therefore show pupils that we value their questions by encouraging them to ask and by responding appropriately.

Task 1

Responding to pupils' questions is much more complex than may be assumed. The approach we probably should be taking is 'situational' – that is, the way we react should be based on an assessment of the best course of action for a particular situation.

❶ What do you usually do when a pupil asks for clarification?

☐ I repeat the question and address it.

☐ I address the question by conversing with that pupil only.

☐ I repeat the question and ask whether anyone in class can provide the answer.

☐ I elicit answers from other pupils and repeat or rephrase them.

☐ Other: _____

It depends on: _____

❷ Where are you positioned when you answer questions?

☐ I stand next to the pupil who asked the question.

☐ I move to a spot in the classroom where everyone can see me.

☐ It depends on: _____

❸ Do you think some of these options make a difference? Why?

❹ How do you make sure that pupils are satisfied with your handling of questions?

Task 2

Pupils often ask questions we are unable to answer, and sometimes they challenge the answers we do give. Teachers are often puzzled about what to do in such situations, and some inexperienced teachers or those lacking in self-confidence try to come up with any response they can, even if they are not certain that it is correct.

❶ What do you think is the best course of action when a pupil asks a question a teacher does not know how to answer?

☐ Teachers should admit that they don't know the answer.

☐ Teachers should tell their pupils that they don't know but will find out.

☐ Teachers should tell their pupils that they don't know but will find out, and should do so as soon as possible.

☐ Teachers should come up with an answer to avoid 'losing face.'

☐ Teachers should pretend they have not heard the question or should ignore it.

☐ Other: _____

❷ What is your own usual reaction in this situation? Does it match what you consider to be the best course? Why or why not?

Task 3

Our pupils' questions and comments can take our lessons in entirely unexpected directions. By adopting a positive approach to unexpected developments, we can turn them into learning experiences; if our attitude is negative, they cause nothing but stress and frustration. The next time something unexpected happens in your class, try to monitor how you react and what you do.

❶ Describe the situation.

❷ What did you do? How do you feel about the way you dealt with the event?

❸ In general, how do you account for spontaneous instruction? What is your rationale?

Task 4

The way pupils respond in class discussions can give us ideas for new teaching directions or mini-lessons on particular topics. We should try to be attentive to pupils' needs and interests, even if they are expressed in unplanned ways.

❶ To what extent do you incorporate flexibility into your lesson plans?

❷ Analyse a video-tape of your teaching. How did you make the most of unplanned situations?

Summary

In this chapter you have considered how you ask questions and how you answer questions from your pupils. You should have been able to determine your strengths and weaknesses in this area and highlight areas for improvement. Copies of your responses to these tasks along with annotated lesson plans, pupil and colleague comments and audio- or video-tapes of lessons and the observation comments of peers and management can be used in your professional development record as evidence of your continuing professional development in this area.

The role of motivation in both learning and teaching cannot be overestimated. There have been many attempts to study and classify the factors involved in motivation. For some time a distinction between 'integrative' and 'instrumental' motivation enjoyed wide popularity – the former being motivation spurred by a need and desire to integrate and identify with a community and the latter arising from a desire to acquire skills or knowledge to use as a tool for achieving other goals. Integrative motivation was thought to be somewhat stronger and longer lasting, though studies in this area have proved quite inconclusive.

Another popular division is between 'intrinsic' motivation that stems from a desire to fulfil personal needs, goals, or ambitions without the promise of a specific reward and 'extrinsic' motivation that comes from the desire to obtain such rewards. Here, intrinsic motivation is thought to be the more powerful.

Common sense supports the idea that accomplishment is one of the best motivators. When we have tangible evidence that we are achieving goals or are effective in what we are doing, motivation increases and is sustained over periods of time. Failure, on the other hand, is a negative experience that often results in loss of motivation. In education, these ideas hold true for both pupils and teachers. If teachers are content with the results of their work, they will embrace their next assignment with more enthusiasm and greater motivation. Similarly, pupils who experience success in school will be more eager to participate and expand their knowledge. Needless to say, the lack of results becomes a burden for both teachers and pupils.

This chapter focuses on pupil and teacher motivation from a broad and practical point of view rather than theoretical one, in an attempt to assist readers in identifying teacher and learner qualities and how they contribute to relationships in the classroom.

Pupil motivation

It seems logical to see motivation as a spectrum of complex, varied, and individualised factors. Generally, however, we might describe a motivated pupil as one who is:

- willing to engage in all learning tasks;
- interested in all aspects of the subject matter;
- eager to cooperate with the teacher and classmates;
- ready to invest energy in the assigned tasks;
- willing to pursue independent learning outside of class;
- able to stay on task;
- willing to encourage classmates to work conscientiously;
- ready to provide suggestions on how the lesson could be improved; and
- able to ask relevant questions about the content being taught.

Task 1

1 Which of the following factors do you think is most important for learning?

☐ Hard work

☐ Aptitude

☐ Persistence

☐ Motivation

☐ Other: _____

2 If a learner lacks one of the factors listed above, can she or he compensate with another? If so, can you think of any pupils whose cases illustrate this point?

Pupil's name	Factor missing	Compensating factor
_____	_____	_____
_____	_____	_____
_____	_____	_____
_____	_____	_____

3 Rank order the descriptors that provide the most relevant conclusion to the following statement: 'In order to learn best, pupils need to be...'

relaxed	motivated	rested
hardworking	interested	comfortable
patient	involved	other:_____

4 How do you capitalise on these qualities among your learners?

Task 2

If pupils have satisfying learning experiences, that feeling of satisfaction and accomplishment motivates them to study further. One of our roles, therefore, is to ensure that initial learning experiences are as positive as possible.

1 Provide an example for each of the ways you have enhanced pupil motivation in recent lessons.

Way of enhancing motivation	Example
I set objectives that are relevant to pupils' personal goals.	_____
I appeal to pupils' need and desire to explore and learn.	_____
I involve pupils in selecting activities, materials, and tasks.	_____
I appeal to pupils' interests.	_____

I offer pupils a lot of positive feedback and encouragement.

_____

I design tasks that enable learners to experience a sense of accomplishment.

_____

I match tasks to the proficiency levels of individual pupils.

_____

Other:

_____

❷ Monitor pupil motivation during your next week of teaching. For each of the activities you plan, rate the level of motivation you expect on a scale from 1 (low) to 5 (high). After the activity is complete, rate the actual level of motivation you observed.

Activity	Expected motivation	Actual motivation	Conclusions
_____	_____	_____	_____
_____	_____	_____	_____
_____	_____	_____	_____
_____	_____	_____	_____
_____	_____	_____	_____
_____	_____	_____	_____

❸ Select an activity for which the expected and actual levels of motivation differed significantly. Survey your pupils on their feelings about the activity.

☐ Did they understand its purpose?

☐ Did they find it useful?

☐ Was it aimed at the appropriate proficiency level?

☐ Did they feel the timing for the activity was reasonable?

☐ Was it relevant to their circumstances and goals?

☐ Did they enjoy working on the task?

❹ Analyse pupils' answers to see if they suggest factors that may have influenced their level of motivation. What conclusions can you draw?

Task 3

❶ The factors that motivate pupils are quite personal. What have you been able to find out about these factors for your current group of pupils?

❷ Identify one of your pupils who lacks motivation, and try to determine what could be done to alter the situation.

Pupil's name: _____

Reasons for lack of motivation (if known): _____

_____

Course of action: _____

_____

Task 4

Inquiring about pupils' interests, hobbies, leisure activities, and goals has a twofold advantage: it shows your genuine interest in your pupils, and it can serve as a basis for planning future activities. If we build schemes of work around materials and topics of interest to our pupils, we can capitalise on the increased motivation that is likely to result.

How much do you know about your pupils? Create a table to list personal details for each pupil, under headings such as 'Interests,' 'Hobbies/Leisure activities,' and 'Goals.' Gather information to complete the chart as you monitor classroom communication or interview pupils, or pass the chart around and ask your pupils to fill it out. Do any common themes emerge? Could you design some upcoming activities to relate to these themes?

Task 5

Pupils are usually motivated at the beginning of a school year. They have high expectations, and the level of motivation they are able to sustain is directly proportional to the level at which their expectations come true. In primary or secondary school settings where there is a 'captive audience,' decreases in motivation can lead to an unpleasant atmosphere for learning and teaching. With older pupils, there may also be an increase in lateness or truancy.

What do you do to ensure that pupils' expectations are met to the largest possible degree? What effect do you feel this has on motivation?

Task 6

❶ What do you do to encourage attendance and punctuality?

	Always				Never
	5	4	3	2	1
I praise pupils who arrive on time.	☐	☐	☐	☐	☐
I take the register at the beginning of the lesson.	☐	☐	☐	☐	☐
I comment on lateness.	☐	☐	☐	☐	☐
I ensure that, in classes of adult students, everyone is aware of special considerations in place when childcare or work schedules conflict with punctuality and attendance.	☐	☐	☐	☐	☐
I try to find out the reasons for lateness or absenteeism.	☐	☐	☐	☐	☐
I 'sum up' attendance periodically and convey the results to pupils.	☐	☐	☐	☐	☐
I am punctual and begin my lessons on time.	☐	☐	☐	☐	☐
I begin each class with an interesting activity.	☐	☐	☐	☐	☐
Other: _____	☐	☐	☐	☐	☐

❷ Pupils may be more inclined to attend regularly if they know what they may be missing. How do you ensure that pupils are aware of upcoming course content?

☐ I provide pupils with a comprehensive list of long-range objectives.

☐ I talk about future lesson plans and activities.

☐ Other: _____

❸ If possible, video-tape the first half-hour of your class for two or three days. Play back the tape and write a description of what happens when pupils arrive late. Is there room for change?

❹ Devise an action plan of what you can do to increase pupil motivation and prevent lateness and absenteeism.

Teacher qualities

Teacher qualities and traits are like genes: each teacher has a unique combination that sets him or her apart from all others. If you think back to your own teachers and compare their qualities, you will certainly agree with this statement. You will also agree that a teacher's qualities have a great deal to do with how motivated pupils are to do their best in class.

Task 1

❶ From the list below, circle the five adjectives that best describe you as a teacher.

interesting	solid	loving
stimulating	reliable	neat
engaging	patient	modest
exciting	motivated	sensitive
enthusiastic	gentle	principled
imaginative	friendly	considerate
hardworking	cheerful	devoted
creative	firm	flexible
encouraging	consistent	precise
caring	decisive	sensible
warm	sympathetic	self-directed
outgoing	organised	innovative
emphatic	stubborn	rational
committed	pleasant	understanding

❷ What does your selection tell you?

❸ What other qualities might you add to this list?

❹ Are there any characteristics listed which you would like to develop further? Devise an action plan for this.

Task 2

While in the classroom, we are constantly observed by our pupils, who examine not only our work but every detail of our appearance. This makes some teachers (especially beginners) believe that appearance contributes to effectiveness.

❶ Have you ever thought about this? How important do you think appearance is, compared to other factors?

❷ Do you think your pupils have certain expectations related to your attire? What are they?

❸ How do you feel on the first day with a new group of pupils, when they actually do seem to focus on the way you look, talk, and behave?

Teacher motivation and attitude

It is generally accepted that our attitude toward teaching has a significant influence in the classroom. It accounts to some degree not only for our own teaching successes and weaknesses, but can also affect pupils' learning. Attitudes seem to generate attitudes: the attitudes we have toward our teaching induce pupils' attitudes and behaviours.

Task 1

Reflect on your commitment and attitude.

❶ Overall, how would you rate your commitment to your pupils?

| 5 | 4 | 3 | 2 | 1 |

Highly committed   Could be more committed

❷ Try to remember your former teachers. What were the qualities and attitudes of those you particularly liked and thought of as effective?

❸ What were the qualities and attitudes of teachers you did not like and did not view as effective?

Personal: _____

Professional: _____

❹ What conclusions can you draw?

Task 2

Classroom behaviours can be a direct result of teacher and pupil attitudes. Think about your own teaching style while you complete the questions in this task.

❶ List some teacher behaviours to which pupils respond positively, and a few that they dislike or would not approve of.

Effective behaviour	Ineffective behaviour
Well prepared for class.	*Unprepared and improvises.*
Keeps notes, teaching materials, and plans well organised.	*Disorganised*

❷ What are some things your pupils praise you for? Do any of your actions give them cause to complain?

❸ Do you think your pupils have clear ideas about how you should behave? If so, how would they define them?

❹ How do pupils react when teachers do not meet their expectations?

❺ You may have talked with your pupils about their responsibilities – perhaps even creating a list of them to post in the classroom – but have you ever created a list of your own responsibilities to share with your pupils?

Yes ☐   No ☐

❻ How useful do you think such a list would be? If you do not have such a list, create one and post it in your classroom. Be sure your pupils are aware of it, and try to stand by the items you list. What do you observe?

Task 3

The word *enthusiastic* in the context of education evokes an image of a pleasant learning atmosphere, with teachers radiating energy and joy for everything they do. Enthusiasm guarantees teachers' profound commitment and attachment to their job and a positive way of dealing with stress. In general, it seems that teachers who have this positive characteristic outside the classroom bring it inside as well.

❶ How enthusiastic are you about what you are doing?

5	4	3	2	1
Very enthusiastic			Not enthusiastic	

❷ Are you happy with what you do?

Yes ☐   No ☐   I don't know ☐

❸ Is there a positive and supportive link between your personal and professional lives?

Yes ☐   No ☐   I don't know ☐

4 How would you rate your overall attitude toward teaching?

5	4	3	2	1
Positive				Negative

5 If possible, video-tape yourself while teaching. How enthusiastic and motivated do you appear to be? Does the tape show something different from the response you gave to question 1?

Task 4

Certain teacher qualities seem to be prerequisite for achieving peak performance within certain teaching settings.

1 In your opinion, what are the most important qualities for any teacher? And what are the most important qualities for teachers of learners of various ages?

Qualities important in any setting	Qualities important for teaching adults	Qualities important for teaching secondary pupils	Qualities important for teaching primary pupils
_____	_____	_____	_____
_____	_____	_____	_____
_____	_____	_____	_____
_____	_____	_____	_____
_____	_____	_____	_____

2 How has the fact that you teach a certain age group influenced your life, your professional development, and your career in general? Which of your qualities has it enhanced?

3 Do you enjoy teaching the age group you teach? What are the positives and negatives?

Your overall well-being

Most (or maybe all?) teachers work in highly stressful environments. Common complaints focus on the enormous workload, problems with pupil behaviour, anxiety over not knowing what the future holds, and difficulty coping with extra responsibilities. Considering the magnitude of the problem and the fact that working conditions rarely change, it is essential that teachers be provided with support to cope with the existing situation. Unfortunately, in most contexts there is not enough done to help teachers ease the stress. Instead, teachers have to develop their own coping strategies, with possibilities including the following:

- adapting to a higher level of tolerance;
- avoiding stressful situations completely or whenever possible;
- changing schools;
- resigning or taking early retirement;
- changing professions; or
- developing techniques to cope with stress (exercise, meditation, etc.).

You will probably agree that the last option is by far the most constructive, but at the same time it may be the most difficult to implement.

Task 1

❶ Many would agree that stress is caused not only by circumstances themselves but by the way we react to them. How do you react to stress and cope with it? Are you satisfied with the results of your approach?

Stressful situation	How do you feel?	How do you usually react?	Does your reaction help alleviate the stress?
_____	_____	_____	_____
_____	_____	_____	_____
_____	_____	_____	_____
_____	_____	_____	_____
_____	_____	_____	_____

❷ If you work in a highly stressful setting and as a consequence are not enthusiastic about what you do, can you identify the factors that contribute to this situation? Indicate the degree of stress caused by each factor.

Factor	Result
_____	_____
_____	_____
_____	_____
_____	_____
_____	_____

❸ Which of the preceding factors are within your power to change?

❹ There are numerous books on coping with stress. What techniques do they usually offer? Would they work for you?

❺ Many people affirm the 'power of positive thinking'. A secondary teacher we know created a positive statement – 'I am confident that I can be fully in charge of my current group of pupils' – and repeated it to herself daily with what she claimed were very positive results. Create your own statement, and try out this method to see if it works for you. What are your observations?

Statement: _____

_____

_____

_____

❻ Another way of easing stress is by helping others. Think about your past teaching week. Did you do anything that made a difference for anyone? Are you planning to help any of your colleagues with anything they find challenging?

Task 2

Allotting some time for your favourite leisure activities and giving yourself the opportunity to 'recharge' is equally important as allotting time, effort, and attention to your family, friends, pupils, and professiona assignments.

❶ How do you usually feel before and after each lesson and at the end of the day?

_____

_____

❷ Do you give yourself periods of peace and quiet during your teaching day?

❸ Do you feel that you don't have enough time for yourself? Is your life 'all work and no play'? If so, monitor your daily schedule for about a week, noting time spent on activities not related to your work or on necessary domestic tasks. Is there a good balance between your work and leisure activities?

Day	Leisure activity	Workload
Monday	_____	_____
Tuesday	_____	_____
Wednesday	_____	_____
Thursday	_____	_____
Friday	_____	_____
Saturday	_____	_____
Sunday	_____	_____

❹ What can you conclude from the preceding chart?

Task 3

At the end of their first year, teachers usually fall into one of two categories: they either feel good about themselves and admire their knowledge (and are sometimes unaware of how much there is still to be learned!) or they feel gloomy about their work and believe they may not be suited to the job. Like everyone, teachers can be very harsh critics of themselves.

How did you feel about your qualities and accomplishments as a teacher at the end of your first year? How do you feel about them today?

Teacher–pupil relationships

The teacher–pupil relationship is not uncommonly a special one, and one that may resonate throughout a lifetime. Pupils often recognise former teachers as 'theirs,' even after many years have passed, and award them a special place in their memories.

Pupils of all ages respond positively to teachers who show interest in and respect for them as individuals, and who provide all the support they need. This attitude in the classroom creates not only a positive learning environment but a positive life experience.

Task 1

❶ Analyse the relationship you develop with your pupils. Video- or audio-tapes of your teaching may help as you complete this task.

	Always				Not at all
	5	4	3	2	1

Awareness of pupils:

	5	4	3	2	1
I know the names of all my pupils.	☐	☐	☐	☐	☐
I know the family situations of all my pupils.	☐	☐	☐	☐	☐
I enquire about pupils' personal accomplishments and interests.	☐	☐	☐	☐	☐
My pupils with visual or aural impairments are seated close to the board or to the position from which I most often teach.	☐	☐	☐	☐	☐
I dress according to my pupils' expectations.	☐	☐	☐	☐	☐

Classroom interaction:

	5	4	3	2	1
I always greet my pupils and acknowledge their presence.	☐	☐	☐	☐	☐
I always smile when greeting them.	☐	☐	☐	☐	☐
I try to create a friendly, supportive, and non-threatening atmosphere.	☐	☐	☐	☐	☐
I tell and listen to jokes and stories.	☐	☐	☐	☐	☐
I often point out the humorous side of a situation.	☐	☐	☐	☐	☐
I try to make my pupils laugh as often as I can.	☐	☐	☐	☐	☐
I have a compassionate, warm, but firm attitude toward pupils.	☐	☐	☐	☐	☐
I use small talk before and after class.	☐	☐	☐	☐	☐
I try to make each of my pupils feel important.	☐	☐	☐	☐	☐
I use gestures and body language to enliven the class.	☐	☐	☐	☐	☐
I display enthusiasm and humour.	☐	☐	☐	☐	☐
I project confidence, strength, and optimism.	☐	☐	☐	☐	☐

Support:

	5	4	3	2	1
I am willing to help pupils during breaks, but I make them aware that I need some rest time, too.	☐	☐	☐	☐	☐
I am an active listener and try to see the other person's point of view, using the information gained to respond effectively.	☐	☐	☐	☐	☐
I show sensitivity to pupils' developmental levels and cultural backgrounds.	☐	☐	☐	☐	☐
I help pupils organise their new knowledge.	☐	☐	☐	☐	☐
I let pupils operate equipment and distribute materials.	☐	☐	☐	☐	☐
I help pupils develop strategies for learning and communication.	☐	☐	☐	☐	☐
In general, I am willing to go out of my way for others.	☐	☐	☐	☐	☐

❷ What are your particular strengths and weaknesses, as revealed by the preceding chart? What can you do to correct the weaknesses?

Task 2

Conduct an experiment: dedicate one of your teaching days to studying your pupils' emotions, both while you teach and as they do classroom activities.

❶ Are your pupils worried, anxious, happy, unhappy, frustrated, joyful, relaxed or…? Look at their faces. Are they smiling, laughing, frowning?

❷ What do their emotions tell you?

❸ Do you see any signs of personal problems among the pupils? If so, what do you view as your role in this situation?

❹ Can these observations help you in any way? How? Is there anything you need to do?

Task 3

In many cultures, teachers are perceived as authorities and are addressed with the highest possible level of respect. If you teach adults who have been exposed to such educational systems, this fact needs to be taken into consideration. For example, many may be uncomfortable being addressed by their first name and may not want to address those in 'authority' in this way.

❶ How do your pupils address you? How do you address them? How do they address each other? Do you sense any discomfort on their part over this issue?

❷ How do you address your colleagues and line managers? How do they address you?

❸ To what extent do forms of address matter in your teaching context?

Task 4

Think about the way you react to events in your classroom.

❶ Try to recall an incident when your pupils pleasantly surprised you. What did they do? What was your reaction?

❷ Recall an incident when your pupils did something you found irritating. How did you react? Did you make them aware of the problem? How?

❸ Would you react the same way again? Why?

Summary

In this chapter you have reflected on the motivation levels of yourself and your pupils. You have also considered ways to improve motivation and attitude. This chapter has also prompted reflection on how you as a teacher deal with stressful situations and how you might cope better with stress. Copies of your responses to these tasks, audio- or video-tapes of lessons and the observation comments of peers and management can be used in your professional development record as evidence of your continuing professional development in this area.

What do you do in response to your pupils' performance? Do you smile, look serious, or maybe frown and shake your head? Do you offer lavish praise? Do you chastise pupils for forgetting a previous lesson or punish by assigning a bad mark? Do you acknowledge good responses with a nod or dismiss them with a shrug, evaluate them or ignore them altogether? All of these options fall into the category of feedback.

Most often feedback is provided orally or in writing, but it can also be expressed in non-verbal forms through body language, gestures, or facial expressions. It can be negative or positive, and can relate to aspects of either the content or form of a pupil's production or performance. If that production or performance is lacking in some way, the teacher's feedback may be offered as *correction*.

This chapter explores various effective techniques for giving feedback and correction and highlights how teachers go about making appropriate choices. We also discuss common problems in this area.

Positive and negative feedback

Picture this scenario: You volunteer to do a special task for your headteacher. In order to complete it, you have to put in considerable effort and work extra hours. When it is finished, you are certain you have done an excellent job. Full of enthusiasm, you stop by the head's office with expectations that your work will be well received. Instead, she barely acknowledges it, much less offers you credit or praise.

Lack of recognition for hard work hurts immensely and has a highly negative influence on motivation. Unfortunately, it can be experienced anywhere. To ensure that it does not occur in your own classroom, consider how you offer feedback by completing the following tasks.

Task 1

How do you provide feedback for both correct and incorrect responses? Your answers to the following questions will be more accurate and objective if you are able to video-tape a few lessons and complete this task after watching the tapes.

❶ Note in point form several instances of feedback you offered in response to both correct (column 1) and incorrect (column 3) responses from pupils (e.g., nodded and said, 'Well done!'; shook my head, saying, 'Anyone else?'). Rate each action by entering a number from 1 (not effective) to 5 (very effective) in the adjacent column.

Feedback to correct response	Rating	Feedback to incorrect response	Rating

Feedback to correct response	Rating	Feedback to incorrect response	Rating
_____	_____	_____	_____
_____	_____	_____	_____
_____	_____	_____	_____

❷ Does one column contain considerably more entries or do you have a good balance? If one is longer, why do you think this is the case?

❸ For each of the following examples of corrective feedback, try to come up with wording that might be more effective or appropriate.

Example   **Your wording**

No, that's not correct.   _____

Not exactly.   _____

No... Does someone have a better answer?   _____

Is that your answer?   _____

You'd better think again.   _____

Pardon? What did you just say?   _____

❹ Corrective feedback starting with the word 'No' may serve only to create barriers, especially for adult learners or pupils with low self-esteem. Discuss the preceding list of examples with your pupils. What wording do they prefer?

❺ Can you think of ways that your feedback techniques could be made more effective?

Task 2

❶ What type of oral feedback do you offer most often?

☐ Feedback on content (what is said or written)   ☐ Feedback on form (how it is said or written)

❷ When you offer feedback, do you give the pupil an opportunity to use that feedback to improve performance? If so, how?

❸ Rank order the type of feedback you provide, according to frequency.

Feedback on writing skills	Feedback on speaking skills
Feedback on listening comprehension	Feedback on reading comprehension
Feedback on language structures used	Feedback on vocabulary use
Feedback on class participation	Feedback on behaviour
Feedback on progress	Feedback on use of strategies that have been taught
Feedback on mistakes	Feedback on content learned

Other: _____

④ Is there any type of feedback listed above that you never or hardly ever provided? If so, why?

⑤ Try to recall your own experience as a pupil. How often were you praised by your teachers? When and how were you criticised? How did these occurrences make you feel? What conclusions can you draw for your own teaching situation?

Task 3

While positive feedback motivates pupils and improves performance, too much negative feedback or a complete lack of feedback can raise barriers to learning. Experienced teachers seem to be able to balance positive and negative feedback, and can see pupils' accomplishments even when they are obscured by errors. They have a sixth sense for providing corrective feedback in a manner that does not discourage pupils but rather helps them see that they can learn from mistakes.

❶ What do you do when offering oral feedback to your pupils?

I provide positive feedback by praising and acknowledging pupils' performance, progress, hard work, commitment, etc.

Yes ☐   No ☐   Sometimes ☐

I acknowledge pupils' contributions to my class and feedback related to my teaching that they provide.

Yes ☐   No ☐   Sometimes ☐

I offer constructive criticism, ensuring that I begin on a positive note.

Yes ☐   No ☐   Sometimes ☐

I make generalised criticisms.

Yes ☐   No ☐   Sometimes ☐

I make blanket statements.

Yes ☐   No ☐   Sometimes ☐

I react negatively.

Yes ☐   No ☐   Sometimes ☐

❷ Which of these teacher behaviours did you find most irritating when you were a pupil?

Task 4

Providing pupils with well-balanced and effective written feedback is a real art. To find out what is involved and to assess your mastery, photocopy some random samples of pupil work that you have evaluated with written comments. (Since we all seem to see things more objectively after some time has passed, it is a good idea to select assignments you marked at least ten days previously.) Analyse the wording of your comments and the manner in which the feedback was provided. Also, check whether you made any mistakes in your corrections.

Your comment/feedback	Could it have been worded differently? How?
_____	_____
_____	_____
_____	_____
_____	_____
_____	_____
_____	_____

Task 5

It is important that we offer written corrective feedback on written work. Reflect on the written feedback you provide.

1 What do you correct?

☐ All mistakes.

☐ Selected mistakes.

☐ It depends on: _____

2 What criteria do you use to determine what and how much to correct?

☐ Pupils' level of proficiency.

☐ Stage in the year (beginning, middle, or end).

☐ Curriculum goals (creative writing, revision work, grasp of concepts, skills, etc.).

☐ Other: _____

3 Do you provide corrections or simply cross out errors?

4 Do you provide a balance of encouragement and correction, or do you tend to focus more on either positive or negative feedback?

5 Do you discuss your feedback with pupils? Why or why not?

6 Do you summarise feedback for individual pupils and provide suggestions related to aspects of their work they need to improve?

Summary

In this chapter you have considered how you provide feedback for your pupils. You have also reflected on how your current practice affects the learning and self-esteem of your pupils. You should have identified your strengths and weaknesses in this area and highlighted areas for improvement. Copies of your responses to these tasks along with pupil and colleague comments and audio- or video-tapes of lessons and the observation comments of peers and management can be used in your professional development record to provide evidence of your continuing professional development in this area.

The terms *assessment, evaluation* and *testing* have considerably different connotations across the literature. This chapter is mainly concerned with assessment as defined by Chris Kyriacou in *Essential Teaching Skills*:

> In essence, assessment is any activity used to appraise pupils' performance. The learning outcomes promoted by schools involve helping pupils to develop knowledge, understanding, skills and attitudes. Assessment thus consists of techniques you can use to monitor pupils' progress in terms of specific learning outcomes.

The most important point to bear in mind when considering assessment is what purpose the assessment activity has. Assessment can serve a number of different purposes, to provide feedback about pupils' progress, to provide pupils with feedback, to provide a record of progress and to provide evidence of teacher and school effectiveness being just a few.

Some assessments will be *formative*, that is they are designed to provide information about a pupil's progress to facilitate effective future learning. This type of assessment is more informal and may involve identifying errors or weaknesses and providing advice and strategies for improvement. Other assessments will be *summative*, to identify the standard of achievement at a particular time, normally at the end of a term or unit of study. Examples of this are the external SATs tests at the end of each key stage or the results of external examinations such as GCSEs.

Within the assessment system in the UK pupils are formally tested in some subjects at the end of each key stage to determine their level of attainment. In addition to this teachers will be expected to maintain records of their pupils' progress and use this information to facilitate learning. This chapter provides opportunities for you to re-examine your testing methods, marking and overall assessment of pupils, and offers ideas on how to encourage pupils to self-assess.

Testing

Most pupils (and many teachers) have quite ambivalent feelings about tests. They dread or claim to hate them, but at the same time they demonstrate curiosity about results, waiting anxiously to see their marks or asking repeatedly when the results will be given to them.

Tests seem to be a necessary tool, used for a variety of purposes: to determine proficiency levels to guide initial pupil placement, to measure progress throughout a course, to identify particular problem areas where pupils may need extra help, and, at the end of a term or year, to determine how well pupils have met objectives. Such tests are often referred to as 'formal'.

Task 1

Placement tests are used to determine pupils' general proficiency at the beginning of a course for the purposes of placing them in appropriate groups and tailoring instruction to a particular proficiency level.

1 In many courses, a formal placement test is used in conjunction with informal assessment to guide decisions about grouping for instruction. On the basis of an initial placement test, pupils are divided into different classes; then, during the first few classes, teachers have a chance to reassess proficiency levels based on classroom interaction and participation and can recommend movement of particular pupils.

How do you reassess pupils during the first few classes? How do you use the results of that assessment?

Task 2

Some tests are administered during a course to determine pupils' progress. They may also be used for diagnostic purposes to point out to pupils and the teacher areas that need attention. Achievement tests are administered at the end of a course to determine how pupils have met curriculum objectives.

1 Consider the methods and techniques of testing that you use in order to determine pupil progress or how well the pupils have met curriculum objectives. What skills and areas do you test?

2 How do the skills and areas you test correspond to what you teach?

3 Do you test certain subskills within each of the skills (e.g., scanning and skimming within the area of reading)?

4 What testing techniques do you use? Circle those you rely on most heavily.

essay questions	unscrambling
short-answer questions	cloze
multiple-choice questions	interviews
true–false statements	role-plays
free writing	story retelling
guided writing	audio- or video-taping
sentence construction	student presentations
paraphrasing	problem-solving
sentence combining	completion of specific tasks
sentence completion	other: _____
fill in the blanks	

5 Discuss the methods you use with your colleagues. Do they use any techniques that you do not? If so, try them out and take notes on how they work.

6 Are your tests designed primarily to indicate what pupils have already learned or to diagnose what they still need to learn?

Task 3

The best tests not only give us information about our pupils and courses, but they also serve as effective learning tools.

❶ To ensure that pupils find your tests useful, do you ask them for feedback? Why or why not? If you do, what procedures do you use?

❷ How do you ensure that pupils benefit as much as possible from the tests you give them?

	Always				Never
	5	4	3	2	1
I design tests so that the majority of pupils will be reasonably successful at them.	☐	☐	☐	☐	☐
I go through the answers in class.	☐	☐	☐	☐	☐
When I mark tests I indicate correct answers so that pupils can see where they went wrong.	☐	☐	☐	☐	☐
I mark tests clearly and provide positive feedback.	☐	☐	☐	☐	☐
I have pupils self-correct tests or exchange tests with a friend for marking.	☐	☐	☐	☐	☐
I apologise when a test has been too difficult.	☐	☐	☐	☐	☐
I follow up with extra practice where necessary.	☐	☐	☐	☐	☐
I mark tests promptly so pupils still remember what each one was about and are motivated to learn the correct responses.	☐	☐	☐	☐	☐

❸ Is there anything in your testing practice that needs improvement or that you would like to alter?

Yes ☐　　　No ☐　　　I don't know ☐

❹ In most courses, not just externally examined ones, it can still worthwhile to test at regular intervals to check what pupils have grasped. Tests can cover material taught during a defined time period, and as a follow-up, pupils can work in groups to discuss their answers and provide a rationale for them. This usually generates a great deal of discussion, during which pupils explain how they feel about their responses. Correct answers are then discussed with the whole class.

Have you ever tried this strategy? If so, what were the results? If not, do you think it could be useful?

❺ Another productive strategy for making tests a learning experience rather than a stressful one is to ask pupils, after correct answers have been discussed, to write down items they feel still need more work. Collecting responses and analysing them provides valuable insight into what needs to be reviewed before teaching new items. Have you ever tried this strategy for gaining pupil feedback?

❻ Pupils often complain about 'surprise tests', tests that include items that they did not expect, and tests that take unanticipated formats. How do you prepare pupils for tests without revealing too much information? Do you feel that some element of surprise is useful? If so, to what extent?

Task 4

Analyse the last test you administered and answer the following questions to help you determine your testing strengths and weaknesses.

❶ Did you test what you taught?

Yes ☐   No ☐

❷ Were the instructions short and clear?

Yes ☐   No ☐

❸ Were the pupils familiar with the test format?

Yes ☐   No ☐

❹ Were the pupils given an appropriate length of time to do the test?

Yes ☐   No ☐

❺ Things I did effectively:

Things I did not do effectively:

❻ Repeat this process two or three times until you have analysed several recently administered tests. Are their weaknesses and strengths the same? Is there a pattern? What can you do to make your tests better?

Task 5

If you repeatedly teach the same material and reuse your tests, it may be a good idea to reflect on their effectiveness and completeness from time to time. Next time you teach the course, complete the following chart to identify what you are teaching and what needs to be taught. Then, compare the completed chart to your old tests. Is there anything that needs to be changed, added, or deleted?

Unit/Topic taught	What needs to be tested?	Test question

Task 6

❶ A test that actually measures what it is supposed to measure is said to be 'valid.' For example, a test of listening skills that consists of a very long recorded speech or conversation followed by twenty comprehension questions may not be valid since it may reveal more about pupils' memories than their ability to understand oral language. A test in a practical computer course that asks pupils to describe how to create tables in a word-processing program does little to indicate whether those pupils can effectively use that tool.

Analyse your last two tests and try to determine their validity.

What was the test intended to measure?	What did the test actually measure?
_____	_____
_____	_____
_____	_____
_____	_____
_____	_____

❷ Another concept commonly mentioned in the literature about assessment is test 'reliability.' A test is not reliable if there are significant differences in the marks awarded by different evaluators. If you have a colleague with whom you feel comfortable and who teaches the same content as you do to pupils of similar age and proficiency, conduct an experiment. Before you mark your next test, each of you photocopy the work of four or five of your pupils and provide the other with a copy of those papers. Both of you should then mark your own tests and the ones selected from your colleague's class, and then compare how the other evaluated the work. How do the corrections differ? What are the similarities? What conclusions can you draw? Which test-correction techniques that you currently use work well across tests? Which ones could be improved?

Marking

To determine how pupils are progressing, most teachers use an established system of assessment that involves assigning marks or grades on both quantitative and qualitative measures. It is no wonder that marking is one of the most common topics of conversation among pupils and teachers. What do teachers and pupils have to say about it? Both groups complain most of the time.

We compiled a list of common complaints and sources of frustration related to marking that are frequently heard among teachers and secondary school pupils:

Teachers' complaints	Pupils' complaints
'Pupils expect high marks even when they don't hand in half of their assignments or do not participate in class.'	'Many teachers don't have a carefully thought-out marking scheme, so they're not clear on what elements they are marking in an assignment or on a test. In other words, they should decide what elements are worth how many marks before they start marking.'
'It annoys me when able pupils complain about every half mark.'	'Favouritism hurts. Teachers should mark the tests without looking at the names.'
'Marking is such a time-consuming process that involves full concentration, and when I have time for it at the end of the day, it just drains me.'	'Marking is always one-sided and subjective. Teachers don't care what you think you deserve. Many of them don't even bother to explain why you got the mark.'
'Pupils are sometimes completely unrealistic – they ask for a mark they do not deserve.'	'In order to get a good mark, you always have to do or write what the teacher wants, and adjust your style to the teachers. We never get to do or write what we feel is important.'
'What irritates me most is when parents come in to fight for marks. They don't have a clear picture of who is in class, and they don't know how many other pupils do a considerably better job than their son or daughter.'	'Marking is always unfair so someone in class – usually to the pupils whose tests are corrected when the teacher is already fed up or simply does not have enough time or energy for them.'

Teachers' complaints	Pupils' complaints
'Pupils often bother me for extensions on deadlines, and then they still expect to get high marks despite the fact that they are handing the assignment in late.'	'Even if you complain, you still have to accept the mark the teacher assigns.'
'I have a feeling that I waste too much energy on marking. It's simply not worth it.'	'Teachers don't mark things quickly enough.'
'I am too exhausted to create complicated marking schemes. Based on my experience, I can give a mark without resorting to maths.'	'Many teachers are very inconsistent. Even if they make their expectations clear, they don't adhere to them.'
'It would be ideal to create common criteria for marking every test and use percentages for each of the elements that needs to be marked, but I simply do not have the energy to do that.'	'I don't know how I am progressing or what kind of report I can expect at the end of the term. The teacher never tells me.'
'I have no life because of marking. I loathe it with passion.'	

Task 1

❶ Many marking-related problems can be avoided. Create a list of tips for teachers based on your experience and the degree to which you think the preceding complaints – both teachers' and pupils' – are legitimate.

Marking do's

_____

_____

_____

_____

_____

Marking don'ts

_____

_____

_____

_____

_____

❷ How content are you with your current marking methods? Do you feel that anything needs to be changed? Are there any obstacles to changing your current approach?

Teaching for the test

In some courses and subjects there is considerable emphasis on pupils' taking and passing a standardised test that will determine whether they will be able to pursue particular educational or career goals. Examples include the SATs tests in English, maths and science at KS1, KS2, KS3 and GCSE examinations at KS4.

Teachers preparing pupils for this type of formal test are under great pressure to ensure the success of their pupils, often in a short time span. Similarly, many pupils who have to take these tests find both the preparation and the actual test stressful.

Task 1

❶ If you teach a class with a strong focus on preparing pupils for a test, what is your approach? Place a tick in the appropriate column to indicate your strengths and any areas that may require some attention.

	Strong point	Needs improvement
My course covers all the skills and areas that appear on the test.	☐	☐
I allot a proper amount of time to each skill and area, based on pupils' needs.	☐	☐
After conducting practice tests I help pupils diagnose problem areas.	☐	☐
I teach test-taking skills: predicting, inferring, guessing, reading or listening between the lines, skimming, scanning, etc.	☐	☐
I encourage pupils to monitor their progress by recording their results for each skill after each practice test.	☐	☐

❷ If you indicated that any of these areas need work, what is your action plan for improvement?

Qualitative assessment

Tests are not the only tool teachers can use to assess pupils' proficiency level, monitor progress, and determine the results of their teaching. Techniques of qualitative assessment, often referred to as 'informal testing' (despite the fact that this name downplays their considerable value), are gaining more and more ground as sources of vital information that cannot be obtained by quantitative measures.

Task 1

❶ Which of the following techniques of qualitative assessment do you use?

☐ Classroom observations   ☐ Pupil self-assessment

☐ Interviews   ☐ Group projects

☐ Case studies   ☐ Pupil presentations

☐ Pupil portfolios   ☐ Other:_____

❷ How do you monitor yours pupils' participation in class activities and your students' progress?

❸ How do you keep track of your observations?

❹ Compare your pupils' results on tests with the information you gain through qualitative techniques. What do you glean from the comparison?

❺ Do you keep pupils aware of the results of all your assessments?

Pupil self-assessment

Self-assessment encourages pupils to take responsibility for their own learning and to monitor their own progress.

Task 1

❶ Place a tick next to the techniques you use or encourage your pupils to use to promote self-assessment.

- ☐ Learning journals
- ☐ Self- and peer-marking of tests
- ☐ Peer-correction of written work
- ☐ Questionnaires about their performance related to various aspects of the course
- ☐ Self-assessment forms and grids
- ☐ Action plans to help pupils keep track of course objectives as they are completed
- ☐ A file of pupils' work for their perusal and evaluation
- ☐ Portfolios
- ☐ Peer-evaluation of pupil presentations or projects
- ☐ Other: _____

❷ Ask your pupils to assess themselves according to the points listed below. (You can add more statements to the list or adjust it to your group of pupils.)

	True	Not true
I was present in class every day.	☐	☐
I was always on time.	☐	☐
I was always in class on time after break.	☐	☐
I stayed in class from the beginning of the lesson to the end.	☐	☐
I participated in all class activities.	☐	☐
I participated in all field trips.	☐	☐
I took notes in class.	☐	☐
I asked questions.	☐	☐
I kept my handouts and materials organised.	☐	☐
I did work at home.	☐	☐
I respected my classmates.	☐	☐
I respected the teacher.	☐	☐
Other: _____	☐	☐

❸ Find out how your pupils feel about this kind of self-assessment. How useful do they find it?

❹ How can the results of this survey improve your teaching?

Summary

In this chapter you have considered the way you assess your pupils' progress, the reliability and validity of tests you construct or use for this. You have also reflected on your marking techniques and the way you prepare students for standardised tests. This reflection should have enabled you to consider your strengths and weaknesses in this area and make improvements in your practice. Copies of the answers to the tasks in this chapter as well as annotated copies of tests and pupil work and the comments of colleagues and pupils on these can be used in your professional development record to provide evidence of your continuing professional development in this area.

In the past few decades, evaluation has received increasing attention as integral to the teaching process. Although there are a multitude of definitions and interpretations of the word *evaluation*, there seems to be general agreement about its overall value. In this chapter, we use Nunan and Lamb's understanding of evaluation, as described in *The Self-Directed Teacher*:

> 'Evaluation involves the collection of information for the purposes of deciding what works and what does not work. This information is used to decide what aspects of an educational program should be left alone and what should be changed. A good evaluation will also offer advice on how changes might be brought about (p. 231).'

Like Nunan and Lamb, in this book we also distinguish *evaluation* from *assessment*, a term reserved for descriptions of what students can or cannot do.

A review of the professional literature in this area reveals different approaches to evaluation and numerous dimensions that shape points of view about it. The types of evaluation most commonly mentioned include the following:

- formative – conducted during the course with the purpose of bringing improvement;
- summative – conducted at the conclusion of the course to determine its effectiveness;
- process – focused on how the course works;
- product – focused on whether course goals have been achieved;
- quantitative – including countable bits of information (test results, statistical data);
- qualitative – including more holistic information based on observation, journal entries, etc.;
- outside – conducted by someone other than the teacher (pupils, peers, managers, or Ofsted inspectors; and
- inside – self-evaluation of teachers by teachers, or of pupils by pupils.

Outside and inside evaluation are often equated, respectively, with formal evaluation (conducted by others, especially managers and inspectors) and informal evaluation (conducted by teachers themselves). Today, however, action research is facilitating the formalisation of self-evaluation, which is included increasingly as a component of overall evaluation, so there may no longer be a clear distinction between the two. The same applies to other forms of evaluation: summative evaluation becomes formative when it is used to revise and improve the next 'run' of the course; quantitative information may be analysed from a qualitative perspective.

Course evaluation, then, can be seen as quite broad and inclusive. It may include evaluation of many aspects of the course, may be conducted by different parties both from inside and outside, and may utilise a variety of instruments and procedures. Since the focus of this book is teacher self-evaluation, this chapter concentrates on course and teacher evaluation as done by pupils, by teachers, and by managers.

The truth may hurt (but it helps us learn)

It would be helpful if someone could provide us with ten easy steps to taming our egos but, failing that, we must develop our own strategies and techniques for doing so. This is difficult to accomplish because, quite simply, criticism hurts. But if we do not prepare ourselves mentally to receive constructive criticism with a view to changing our patterns, then conducting a course evaluation will be a waste of time.

Once a teacher does decide to undertake such an evaluation, there are a number of things that must be kept in mind.

- Course evaluation takes courage. Don't do it until you are absolutely ready, or it will only result in frustration for both you and your pupils.
- Prepare yourself to face both positive and negative comments. The positive ones may boost your self-esteem, but it is the negative comments that shed a different light on your perception of your teaching and facilitate the self-improvement process.
- Only constructive criticism helps, so make sure whoever is conducting the evaluation knows what that means.
- Many teachers believe that evaluation often results in loss of face. The truth is that, regardless of the results, your willingness to undertake such an evaluation demonstrates only your very positive desire to improve. This is not a test; there are no wrong answers or bad marks, but just opinions about your teaching viewed from different perspectives.
- In some cultures it is considered completely inappropriate for pupils to evaluate their teachers. If your class includes pupils from such cultures and your evaluation will include solicitation of pupil responses, extra preparation will need to be undertaken to explain the benefits of the evaluation.

Although it is clear that evaluation is beneficial, a great deal of research remains to be done to determine the extent of its value. Since you are holding this book in your hands and are reading this chapter, you are obviously interested in exploring this area. You may be a pioneer whose willingness to undertake evaluation will help us all understand how and why it can contribute to improved teaching practice.

Task 1

A secondary school teacher asked her pupils to evaluate her course at the end of the year. Pupils obviously had a bone to pick with her, and welcomed what they saw as an opportunity to point out her weaknesses. Most of their evaluation sheets revealed the same deficiency: during her lessons, she would immerse herself totally with the weaker pupils and, as a result, other pupils' needs were overlooked; furthermore, because the same tasks were assigned to everyone in the class, stronger pupils often ended up twiddling their thumbs or reading magazines toward the end of lessons. When the teacher read the evaluation sheets, she was terribly upset. She announced that she would never conduct an evaluation in her class again. She commented further that she generally had no problems with criticism, as long as it was not direct criticism of her performance.

What do you think the teacher was trying to accomplish with the survey? What do you think about her level of preparation for it? What does this tell you about the culture of secondary school students?

Evaluation by pupils

No one can provide better feedback on overall course quality than pupils. This may seem obvious but, in practice, it is often overlooked. We tend to forget that pupils can be the best teacher trainers. Their insights and perceptions regarding our lessons, performance, and professionalism can assist us in building clearer and more objective images of the quality of our teaching and in identifying areas that need to be improved.

Task 1

Teachers who ask their pupils for feedback should be prepared for a range of responses – from open, constructive comments on evaluation surveys to negative reactions or signs of disapproval on pupils' faces during lessons.

1. Do you remember any pupil comments – either positive or negative – that have had a profound effect on you, personally or professionally?

2. Try to recall a negative comment. What was it related to?

3. Analyse the action that triggered the negative reaction or comment. Was there anything you could have done differently? Was there anything your pupils should have done differently?

Task 2

Evaluation is most often conducted at the end of a course, when pupils are asked to list positive points, identify problem areas, and suggest changes with the benefit of a clear image of what has been taught, how, and with what results. It seems to us equally valid, however, to obtain pupil feedback as a course gets under way. If you were standing at a junction and were not entirely sure of which road to take, how would you decide which way to go? You might stop a passer-by and ask for directions. At the end of the first few weeks in a school year or term, you may be standing at such a junction, and your pupils are the passers-by who can confirm which route to take in terms of instructional method, classroom atmosphere, and resources and learning materials. They have been exposed to enough of your teaching style and methodology, so they will be able to tell you whether they feel that something needs to be altered to maximise their learning. Their responses are useful for diagnostic purposes and can be the most valuable predictor of how your class will unfold. They may be the eye-opener that prompts you to reorganise the course or to make minor cosmetic changes.

1. Create a list of questions for your pupils that you might use as an interim evaluation.

2. After the first few weeks of your next year or term, pose the questions. What are the results? How do the results affect your thinking about how the course will proceed?

3. Try conducting a similar survey informally and orally, perhaps every week or few days. Ask questions such as 'How do you feel about this? How much more practice do you need? What do you think about this type of activity?' If you are a novice teacher, you could add, 'I've never tried this activity before, and I'd like to know how you feel about it.' Does this sort of informal evaluation have an impact on your lessons and practice? Does expressing this sort of interest in your pupils' learning preferences affect the classroom atmosphere?

Task 3

Conducting a pupil survey at the end of a unit may provide ideas for improvement for the next time you teach the same content. An 'end of the unit' evaluation questionnaire might ask pupils to rate the unit's usefulness and importance, the degree of difficulty of its various components, the elements they found most and least enjoyable, how well its purposes were realised, and how motivated they were by it, and ask pupils' suggestions for improvement.

Design such a questionnaire to solicit pupil evaluation of your next unit. What are the results? Why is undertaking such an evaluation useful? How do the pupils view it?

Supervisory evaluation

Teachers in the UK are becoming increasingly used to being evaluated by senior management, curriculum advisers and Ofsted inspectors. Trainee teachers and NQTs in particular are observed frequently by teacher mentors and others. Complaints about the practice of supervisory observation include those about its anxiety-producing aspects and the fact that it is sometimes considered a waste of time because teachers may 'put on a show' or 'follow the party line' when a supervisory observer is in their classroom. Most of the proponents of supervisory evaluation acknowledge the potential pitfalls but express the belief that observation facilitates the reflective process of professional development and should be conducted with that purpose in mind.

There are two main factors that determine the value of classroom observations for the teacher being observed: the nature of the feedback and the evaluator. Feedback that is detailed, informed and insightful is appreciated and received more positively; the more credible, trusted and knowledgeable the evaluator, the more persuasive and useful the feedback is for the observed teacher.

Task 1

❶ What is your opinion on supervisory evaluation? What do you see as its benefits and disadvantages?

❷ If you feel that the model of supervisory evaluation now in place in your school or department is not effective, how do you think it ought to be changed?

❸ Teachers have often complained that a mandatory evaluation by an Ofsted inspector or adviser is stressful. What strategies can you use to lessen the impact of this on yourself?

Task 2

A teacher's wish-list regarding desirable qualities for an evaluator might include the following:

- the ability to motivate teachers and help them work to their full potential;
- good listening and people skills;
- professionalism;
- expertise and experience; and
- approachability and availability.

1. What additional things would you add to this list? Why?

2. At some point in all of our careers, we have been evaluated formally. How do you feel about your evaluation experiences?

3. Do you have a chance to offer feedback, explanations, or clarifications?

4. Is there anything you would like to change about the way supervisory observations are conducted in your teaching context?

5. How can you facilitate this change?

Task 3

Each of us have had the opportunity in our careers to gain years of classroom teaching practice. Based on our experience, we feel that supervisory evaluation should be guided by these two underlying principles:

- observing effective and ineffective teacher behaviours, learning from them, and then helping others acquire that knowledge; and

- encouraging teachers to self-evaluate and learn from the process.

1. How much of their knowledge do your evaluators share with you? How useful do you find it?

2. Have your managers encouraged you to self-evaluate?

   Yes ☐   No ☐

3. How does 'delivered wisdom' from managers or advisers compare to what you have learned on your own, through the process of self-evaluation?

Summary

In this chapter you have reflected on how you evaluate your course or teaching units through pupil evaluation or through supervisory evaluation. It is hoped that you will have considered the value of such evaluation and how it can inform your professional practice. Pupil evaluations and evaluations by management, colleagues and advisers can be used in your professional development record to demonstrate your capacity for reflective practice and to identify strengths and weaknesses in your teaching and highlight areas in which you require continuing professional development.

The time when one graduated from secondary school, college, or university equipped with all the skills and knowledge necessary for the next thirty or forty years of professional practice is long gone. With new theories and methods continually being developed, questioned, and re-examined, and with science and technology changing at a rapid rate, the need for career-long learning is a reality we all have to accept.

Research or practice?

Do teachers learn more from their own classroom experience and their 'on the spot' experiments and action research than they do from published results of research studies? Is teaching a profession or a trade? A possible answer to these questions is offered by Carr and Kemmis:

> 'One indication of the degree of professionalization of a field is the extent to which the methods and procedures employed by members of a profession are based on a body of theoretical knowledge and research.'

Task 1

❶ Obviously, in our first few years in the classroom, we base our practice on the knowledge gained in teacher preparation courses. Place a tick next to the areas of study that were included in your own initial teacher training.

☐ Discipline-specific knowledge

☐ Classroom-based research

☐ Critical pedagogy

☐ Education for cultural diversity

☐ Curriculum and syllabus design

☐ Assessment

☐ Methodology

☐ Technology in the classroom

☐ Other: _____

❷ If there are any areas that were not covered in your teacher preparation programme, how did you go about gaining knowledge in them? If there are areas with which you are unfamiliar, how could you go about exploring them?

Task 2

As a student and probably at some point in your teaching career, you have had a chance to observe other teachers at work. Some of them may have been excellent, but it is likely that others did not impress you.

Skill in teaching derives from a combination of discipline-specific knowledge and an understanding of pedagogy and methodology, interpersonal skills, and personal qualities. The following table lists Hay McBer's (1999) characteristics of teacher effectiveness. How do you rate each of these?

	Very important			Less important	
	5	4	3	2	1

Professionalism:

Challenge and support: A commitment to do everything possible for each pupil and to enable all pupils to be successful. ☐ ☐ ☐ ☐ ☐

Confidence: The belief in one's ability to be effective and take on challenges. ☐ ☐ ☐ ☐ ☐

Creating trust: Being consistent and fair. Keeping one's word. ☐ ☐ ☐ ☐ ☐

Respect for others: The underlying belief that individuals matter and deserve respect. ☐ ☐ ☐ ☐ ☐

Thinking:

Analytical thinking: The ability to think logically, break things down and recognise cause and effect. ☐ ☐ ☐ ☐ ☐

Conceptual thinking: The ability to see patterns and links, even where there is a lot of detail. ☐ ☐ ☐ ☐ ☐

Planning and setting expectations:

Drive for improvement: Relentless energy for setting and meeting challenging targets, for pupils and the school. ☐ ☐ ☐ ☐ ☐

Information seeking: A drive to find out more and get to the heart of things; intellectual curiosity. ☐ ☐ ☐ ☐ ☐

Initiative: The drive to act now to anticipate and pre-empt events. ☐ ☐ ☐ ☐ ☐

Leading:

Flexibility: The ability and willingness to adapt to the needs of a situation and change tactics. ☐ ☐ ☐ ☐ ☐

Holding people accountable: The drive and ability to set clear expectations and parameters and to hold others accountable for performance. ☐ ☐ ☐ ☐ ☐

Managing pupils: The drive and ability to provide clear direction to pupils, and to enthuse and motivate them. ☐ ☐ ☐ ☐ ☐

Passion for learning: The drive and ability to support pupils in their learning and to help them become confident and independent learners. ☐ ☐ ☐ ☐ ☐

Relating to others:

Impact and influence: The ability and drive to produce positive outcomes by impressing and influencing others. ☐ ☐ ☐ ☐ ☐

Team working: The ability to work with others to achieve shared goals. ☐ ☐ ☐ ☐ ☐

Understanding others: The drive and ability to understand others, and why they behave as they do. ☐ ☐ ☐ ☐ ☐

❷ What are your own strengths? What might you be able to do about any weaknesses?

Professional development options

We have a responsibility to pursue ongoing professional development not only to improve our practice but also the image of our profession. Increasingly teachers are being expected to document and evidence their commitment to continuing professional development. Newly qualified teachers have a career entry profile, threshold payments depend upon evidencing relevant professional development and performance management requires regular appraisals to consider the strengths and weaknesses of a teacher and to formulate an action plan for professional development. The professional development options open to teachers include the following:

- networking through committees, conferences, and workshops;
- membership in professional associations;
- taking courses;
- disseminating good ideas by presenting at workshops, writing articles, and sharing materials;
- staying informed about issues pertaining to the profession and field;
- conducting action research.

Task 1

❶ Which of these options have you used recently?

❷ Professional development is conducted in a multitude of ways. Study the list below and make notes about what you have done or plan to do in future.

Option	Details
Taking courses/workshops	_____
Exploring published research	_____
Reading professional publications	_____
Searching computer databases (e.g., ERIC) or the Internet for information on particular topics	_____
Attending workshops and conferences	_____
Participating in 'swap shops' to exchange teaching materials and ideas	_____
Participating in inservice activities within your department or school	_____
Reviewing textbooks	_____
Developing new activities	_____
Sharing ideas and materials with colleagues	_____
Visiting resource centres and professional libraries	_____
Conducting self-evaluation or classroom research through action research	_____

peer observation _____

checklists _____

video- or audio-recording your teaching _____

filling out your own observation report
during supervisory evaluation _____

portfolio assessment _____

setting professional development goals
and reflecting on the results _____

Other: _____ _____

_____ _____

_____ _____

_____ _____

❸ In our experience, teacher self-evaluation undertaken simultaneously by staff throughout a school or department is very worthwhile. Participation should be voluntary, but we have found that teachers are often happy to participate if they know that their colleagues will be involved. By using tasks such as those described in this book, self-evaluation can become peer-evaluation, and insights can be shared among colleagues.

Do you think such a project would be feasible in your teaching context? How valuable do you feel it would be? How could it be initiated?

Annual or termly professional growth plans

'Let bygones be bygones' describes some people's philosophy for life, but in our opinion these words should not guide teachers within their professions. On New Year's Eve, many of us reflect back on the passing year, re-evaluate, and make New Year's resolutions. Similarly, at the beginning of a new school year or term, it is valuable for us to reassess our teaching and set goals for professional growth.

Task 1

❶ At the beginning of your next teaching year or term, review the areas in the following table. At the end of the year or term, revisit the table and fill in column 3. Focus on three areas and formulate your growth objectives.

Area	Your objective	Results
Course outline	_____	_____
Daily plans	_____	_____
Handouts	_____	_____
Field trips	_____	_____
Guest speakers	_____	_____

Classroom organisation
and arrangement _____   _____

Communication skills _____   _____

Class events _____   _____

Conferences, workshops _____   _____

New units or topics _____   _____

New resources _____   _____

Teaching skills to monitor _____   _____

Knowledge of the subject
matter _____   _____

Other:_____ _____   _____

❷ How did the results match your objectives? What actions do you plan to take in your next teaching session?

Task 2

A professional development record represents a collection of items that illustrate work accomplished during a school year or term. Teachers are encouraged to include material that represents both successful and unsuccessful teaching, so that ideas for improvement will be revealed along with creativity and strengths. The items may be categorised according to the factors considered relevant for evaluation by the school, department or teacher. They can be reviewed by the teacher alone or by a manager as part of an evaluation or less formal constructive dialogue, or teachers may opt to share their collections with colleagues so that the process will benefit everyone. Supervisory or peer-evaluation of records, if conducted sensitively, provides the opportunity for teachers to share their rationale for particular actions or activities and to exchange advice and suggestions.

Like other techniques, professional development records are most effective for evaluative purposes if they are used in conjunction with other approaches. Completing a checklist related to long-range plans or watching a video of yourself in action in the classroom in order to analyse particular teaching skills could be done alongside the gathering and reviewing of items. The main underlying principle, as with any other self-evaluation technique, is awareness raising.

This task will help you create and monitor a professional development record. At the beginning of the year, designate a file box for your collection. Label it clearly so it will not be accidentally discarded, and put it somewhere easily accessible. Throughout the year or term, gather items related to your class or course and store them in the box. To make the whole process more systematic, prepare a review chart such as the one shown overleaf. Keep the chart in the box, and make a note each time you add an item.

Topic	Item	Reflections
Course outline		
Daily plans		
Handouts		
Pupil work		
'Souvenirs' from field trips		
Materials depicting class events		
Visual aids		
Materials collected at conferences or workshops		
Handouts from guest speakers		
New units, topics developed		
New resources tried out		
Knowledge of the subject matter		
Other:_____		

❶ Toward the end of the year, set up a session for reflection with a colleague or a supervisor. Ask him or her to look through your record while you discuss what you have accomplished, share any concerns, and seek advice. What is the result? What have you learned about the process? What insights have you gained that you can apply in your next teaching session?

❷ Compare your objectives set at the beginning of the session or year and the results revealed by your professional development record. How do the two compare? What conclusions can you draw?

❸ Use your reflections from this task and the preceding one to set up professional development objectives for next year or term.

Summary

This final chapter is intended to pull together the preceding material and provide ideas and reflection on your own professional development as a teacher. Having worked through the chapters you will have reflected on many aspects of your teaching practice and considered ways to improve the teaching and learning in your classroom. As professionals teachers have a duty to continually develop, refine and upgrade their skills and knowledge. Personally committing to planned and systematic continuing professional development will ensure that this happens. This chapter has provided you with the ideas on how to obtain this professional development and how to record and evidence it in a systematic and effective way to enable reflective practice.

Carr, W. and Kemmis, S. (1998) *Becoming Critical: Education, Knowledge and Action Research*. London: Falmer Press.

Freeman, D. (1998) *Doing Teacher Research*. Boston: Heinle & Heinle.

Golebiowska, A. (1990) *Getting Students to Talk* (International English Language Teaching series). Englewood Cliffs, NJ: Prentice Hall.

Harmer, J. (1995) 'Taming the Big "I": Teacher Performance and Student Satisfaction', in *ELT Journal*, vol. 49, no. 4.

Hay McBer, H. (2000) *A Model of Teacher Effectiveness*. Report by Hay McBer to the Department of Education and Employment.

Kyriacou, C. (1998) *Essential Teaching Skills*. Cheltenham: Stanley Thornes.

Moon, R., Butcher, J. and Bird, E. (2000) *Leading Professional Development in Education*. London: Routledge Falmer in association with the Open University.

Nunan, D. and Lamb, C. (1996) *The Self-Directed Teacher*. Cambridge, UK: Cambridge University Press.

Wajnryb, R. (1993) *Classroom Observation Tasks*. Cambridge, UK: Cambridge University Press.

The Department for Education and Skills website provides a wealth of information and guidance:

www.dfes.gov.uk